Continual Service Improvement based on ITIL® V3 - A Management Guide

G000059652

Other publications by Van Haren Publishing

Van Haren Publishing (VHP) specializes in titles on Best Practices, methods and standards within IT management, Architecture (Enterprise and IT), business management and project management.

These publications are grouped in series, eg: *ITSM Library* (on behalf of ITSMF International), *Best Practice* and *IT Management Topics*. VHP is also publisher on behalf of leading companies and institutions, eg The Open Group, IPMA-NL, CA, Getronics, Pink Elephant. At the time of going to press the following books are available:

IT (Service) Management / IT Governance

ITSM, ITIL® V3 and ITIL® V2
Foundations of IT Service Management – based on ITIL® V3 (English, Dutch, German; French, Japanese and Spanish editions)
Introduction to IT Service Management (ITIL V3, English)
IT Service Management based on ITIL V3 – A Pocket Guide (English, Dutch, German, Italian; French, Japanese and Spanish editions)
Foundations of IT Service Management based on ITIL® (ITIL V2), (English, Dutch, French, German, Spanish, Japanese, Chinese, Danish, Italian, Korean, Russian, Arabic; also available as a CD-ROM)
Implementing Service and Support Management Processes (English)
Release and Control for IT Service Management, based on ITIL® – A Practitioner Guide (English)

ISO/IEC 20000
ISO/IEC 20000 – An Introduction (English, German)
Implementing ISO/IEC 20000 Certification (English)
ISO/IEC 20000 – A Pocket Guide (English, Italian, German, Spanish, Portuguese)

ISO 27001 and ISO 17799
Information Security based on ISO 27001 and ISO 17799 – A Management Guide (English)
Implementing Information Security based on ISO 27001 and ISO 17799 – A Management Guide (English)

CobiT
IT Governance based on CobiT4.1® – A Management Guide (English, German, Japanese)

IT Service CMM
IT Service CMM – A Pocket Guide (English)

ASL and BiSL
ASL – A Framework for Application Management (English, German)
ASL – Application Services Library – A Management Guide (English, Dutch)
BiSL – A Framework for Business Information Management (Dutch, English)
BiSL – Business information Services Library – A Management Guide (Dutch; English)

ISPL
IT Services Procurement op basis van ISPL (Dutch)
IT Services Procurement based on ISPL – A Pocket Guide (English)

Other IT Management titles:
De RfP voor IT-outsourcing (Dutch; English version due Spring 2008)
Decision- en Controlfactoren voor IT-Sourcing (Dutch)
Defining IT Success through the Service Catalogue (English)
Frameworks for IT Management – An introduction (English, Japanese; German)
Frameworks for IT Management – A Pocket Guide (English, German, Dutch)
Implementing IT Governance (English)
Implementing leading standards for IT management (English, Dutch)
IT Service Management global best practices, volume 1 (English)
IT Service Management Best Practices, volume 1, 2, 3 and 4 (Dutch)
ITSM from hell! / ITSM from hell based on Not ITIL (English)
ITSMP – The IT Strategy Management Process (English)

Metrics for IT Service Management (English, Russian)
Service Management Process Maps (English)
Six Sigma for IT Management (English)
Six Sigma for IT Management – A Pocket Guide (English)

MOF/MSF
MOF – Microsoft Operations Framework, A Pocket Guide (Dutch, English, French, German, Japanese)
MSF – Microsoft Solutions Framework, A Pocket Guide (English, German)

Architecture (Enterprise and IT)

TOGAF, The Open Group Architecture Framework – A Management Guide (English)
The Open Group Architecture Framework – 2007 Edition (English, official publication of TOG)
TOGAF™ Version 8 Enterprise Edition – Study Guide (English, official publication of TOG)
TOGAF™ Version 8.1.1 Enterprise Edition –A Pocket Guide (English, official publication of TOG)

Business Management

ISO 9000
ISO 9001:2000 – The Quality Management Process (English)

EFQM
The EFQM excellence model for Assessing Organizational Performance – A Management Guide (English)

SqEME®
Process management based on SqEME® (English)
SqEME® – A Pocket Guide (English, Dutch)

Project/Programme/Risk Management

ICB/NCB
NCB Versie 3– Nederlandse Competence Baseline (Dutch, on behalf of IPMA-NL)
Projectmanagement op basis van NCB V3 – IPMA-C en IPMA-D (Dutch)

PRINCE2™
Project Management based on PRINCE2™– Edition 2005 (English, Dutch, German)
PRINCE2™ – A No Nonsense Management Guide (English)
PRINCE2™ voor opdrachtgevers – Management Guide (Dutch)

MINCE®
MINCE® – A Framework for Organizational Maturity (English)

MSP
Programme Management based on MSP (English, Dutch)
Programme Management based on MSP – A Management Guide (English)

M_o_R
Risk Management based on M_o_R – A Management Guide (English)

Other publications on project management:
Wegwijzer voor methoden bij Projectvolwassenheid (Dutch: fall 2008)
Het Project Management Office – Management Guide (Dutch)

For the latest information on VHP publications, visit our website: www.vanharen.net

Continual Service Improvement
based on ITIL® V3

A Management Guide

Van Haren
PUBLISHING

Colophon

Title:	Continual Service Improvement based on ITIL® V3 - A Management Guide
Authors:	Jan van Bon (Chief Editor, Inform-IT)
	Arjen de Jong (co-author, Inform-IT)
	Axel Kolthof (co-author, Inform-IT)
	Mike Pieper (co-author, Inform-IT)
	Ruby Tjassing (co-author, Inform-IT)
	Annelies van der Veen (co-author, Inform-IT)
	Tieneke Verheijen (co-author, Inform-IT)
Copy editor:	Jayne Wilkinson
Publisher:	Van Haren Publishing, Zaltbommel, www.vanharen.net
Design & layout:	CO2 Premedia bv, Amersfoort - NL
ISBN:	9789087531287
Edition:	First edition, first impression, June 2008

© 2008 Van Haren Publishing

Foreword

ITIL receives more and more attention on a global scale, with many companies adopting its principles. In that respect, ITIL version 2 has done a good job. The update of ITIL in version 3, released in June 2007, has caused some concern for many of these companies, since it built on the idea that companies had already achieved results with version 2 content. In practice however, most companies are still working their way through the basic principles of ITIL. For that reason, the "Foundations of IT Service Management - based on ITIL V3" was developed, offering a comprehensive but easy-to-understand source of information on ITIL. This title is now widely used as the authoritative guide on ITIL V3 in training situations and in implementations.

Apart from offering the market a summarized, easy-to-understand source on ITIL V3, that can be used for a step-by-step approach, many companies focus on a subset of the ITIL best practices. That is why we developed a series of ITIL Management Guides, focusing on the processes, procedures, and functions, from each of the phases of the ITIL V3 Lifecycle. This enables companies to focus on those phases that are of primary concern to them.

Each of the five ITIL V3 Management Guides is structured the same way as the successful Foundations book: it separates the Lifecycle information from the single process, procedure and function components, enabling organizations to take their own approach and still adopt ITIL best practices.

The content of each guide was derived from the Foundations book, which ensures that you'll find the same high quality as usual. This means that all content has been peer-reviewed in a rigorous way, making sure that it completely aligns to ITIL V3, but also that it was the best, concise and comprehensive summary of ITIL V3 core content that could be achieved.

I'm convinced that this new management guide will provide an excellent reference tool for practitioners, students and others who want to have a practical guide on the key ITIL V3 concepts.

Jan van Bon
Chief Editor

Acknowledgements

This Management Guide is a compilation of the itSMF publication "Foundations of IT Service Management - Based on ITIL V3". Thus, the international review team that reviewed "Foundations of IT Service Management", has contributed indirectly to this Management Guide. We would like to thank all reviewers once again for their detailed review which improved the quality of both books significantly.

The review team consists of:
- John van Beem, ISES International, Netherlands
- Aad Brinkman, Apreton, Netherlands
- Peter Brooks, PHMB Consulting, itSMF South Africa
- Rob van der Burg, Microsoft, Netherlands
- Judith Cremers, Getronics PinkRoccade Educational Services, Netherlands
- Robert Falkowitz, Concentric Circle Consulting, itSMF Switzerland
- Rosario Fondacaro, Quint Wellington Redwood, Italy
- Peter van Gijn, LogicaCMG, Netherlands
- Jan Heunks, ICT Partners, Netherlands
- Linh Ho, Compuware Corporation, USA
- Ton van der Hoogen, ToTZ Diensten, Netherlands
- Kevin Holland, NHS, UK
- Matiss Horodishtiano, Amdocs, itSMF Israel
- Wim Hoving, BHVB, Netherlands
- Brian Johnson, CA, USA
- Georges Kemmerling, Quint Wellington Redwood, Netherlands
- Kirstie Magowan, itSMF New Zealand
- Steve Mann, OpSys - SM2, itSMF Belgium
- Reiko Morita, Ability InterBusiness Solutions, Inc., Japan
- Jürgen Müller, Marval Benelux, Netherlands
- Ingrid Ouwerkerk, Getronics PinkRoccade Educational Services, Netherlands
- Ton Sleutjes, CapGemini, Netherlands
- Maxime Sottini, Innovative Consulting, itSMF Italy
- Takashi Yagi, Hitachi Ltd., itSMF Japan

Given the desire for a broad consensus in the IT Service Management field, new developments, additional material and contributions from ITSM professionals who have worked with ITIL version 3 are welcome. They will be discussed by the editors and where appropriate incorporated into new editions. Comments can be sent to the Chief Editor, Jan van Bon, email: j.van.bon@inform-it.org.

Contents

x

CHAPTER 1

Introduction

1.1 Background

Developments in IT have had a tremendous effect on the business market during the last decade. Since the appearance of extremely powerful hardware, highly versatile software and super-fast networks, all connected to each other worldwide, organizations have been able to develop their information-dependent products and services to a greater extent, and to bring them to the market much faster. These developments have marked the transition of the industrial age into the **information age**. In the information age, everything has become faster and more dynamic, and everything is connected.

Traditional hierarchical organizations often have difficulties in responding to this rapidly changing market, and this has led to current trends for organizations to become flatter and more flexible. The focus has shifted from vertical silos to horizontal **processes**, and decision-making powers are increasingly bestowed on the employees. It is against this background that the work processes of IT service management have arisen.

An important advantage of process-oriented organizations is that processes can be designed to support a **customer-oriented approach**. This has made the alignment between the IT organization (responsible for supplying information) and the customer (responsible for using these information systems in their business) increasingly significant. Over the last couple of years, this trend has attracted attention under the title of **Business-IT Alignment (BITA)**.

As organizations gained more experience with the **process-oriented approach** of IT service management, it became clear that the process must be managed coherently.

Furthermore, it was obvious that the introduction of a process-oriented work method meant a big change for the primarily line and project-oriented organizations. Culture and change management proved to be crucial elements for a successful organizational design.

Another important lesson learned was that the IT organization must not lose itself in a process culture. Just like the one-sided project-oriented organization, a one-sided process-oriented organization was not the optimum type of business. Balance was, as always, the magic word. In addition, it became clear that the customer-oriented approach required that an **end-to-end** and **user-centric** approach must be followed: it was of no help to the user to know that "the server was still in operation" if the information system was not available at the user's workplace. IT services must be viewed in a larger context. The need for the recognition of the **Service Lifecycle**, and the management of IT services in light of that lifecycle, became a concern.

Due to the fast growing dependency of business upon information, the quality of information services in companies is being increasingly subjected to stricter **internal and external requirements**. The role of **standards** is getting more and more important, and **frameworks** of "best practices" help with the development of a management system to meet these requirements. Organizations that are not in control of their processes, will not be able to realize great results on the level of the Service Lifecycle and the end-to-end-management of those services. Organizations that do not have their internal organization in order, will also not achieve great results. For these reasons, all these aspects are handled alongside each other in the course of this book.

1.2   Why this book

This book offers detailed information for those who are responsible for strategic information issues, as well as for the (much larger) group who are responsible for setting up and executing the delivery of the information systems. This is supported by both the description of the Service Lifecycle, as documented in ITIL version 3, and by the description of the processes that are associated with it. The ITIL core books are very extensive, and can be used for a thorough study of contemporary best practices. This management guide provides the reader with an easy-to-read comprehensive introduction to the broad library of ITIL core books, to support the understanding and the further distribution of ITIL as an industry standard. Once this understanding of the structure of ITIL has been gained, the reader can use the core books for a more detailed understanding and guidance for their daily practice.

1.3 Organizations

Several organizations are involved in the maintenance of ITIL as a description of the "best practice" in the IT service management field.

OGC

Initially ITIL was a product of the CCTA, a UK Government Organization. On 1 April 2001 the CCTA was incorporated into the OGC, which thus became the new owner of ITIL. The aim of the OGC is to help its clients (within the UK Government) with the modernization of their procurement activities and the improvement of their services, by, among other things, making the best possible use of IT: "OGC aims to modernize procurement in government, and deliver substantial value for money improvements". The OGC promotes the use of "best practices" in numerous areas, such as project management, program management, procurement, risk management and IT service management. For this reason the OGC itself has published several series of books (Libraries) which have been written by (international) experts from different companies and organizations.

itSMF

The target group for this publication is anyone who is involved or interested in IT service management. A professional organization, working on the development of the IT service management field, has been created especially for this target group.

In 1991 the Information Technology Service Management Forum (itSMF), originally known as the Information Technology Infrastructure Management Forum (ITIMF), was set up as a UK association. In 1994, a sister-association was established in the Netherlands, following the UK example.

Since then, independent itSMF organizations have been set up in more than forty countries, spread across the globe, and the number of "chapters" continues to grow. All itSMF organizations operate under the umbrella organization, itSMF International (itSMF-I).

itSMF is aimed at the entire professional area of IT service management. It promotes the exchange of information and experiences that IT organizations can use to improve their service provision. itSMF is also involved in the use and quality of the various standards and methods that are important in the field. One of these standards is ITIL. itSMF International has an agreement with OGC and APM Group on the promotion of the use of ITIL.

APM Group

In 2006, OGC contracted the management of ITIL rights, the certification of ITIL exams and accreditation of training organizations to the APM Group (APMG), a commercial organization. APMG defines the certification and accreditation for the ITIL exams, and published the new certification system (see Section 2.1: ITIL exams).

Exam bodies

The Dutch foundation Examen Instituut voor Informatica (EXIN) and the English Information Systems Examination Board (ISEB, part of the BCS: the British Computer Society) cooperated in the development and provision of certification for IT service management. For many years they were the only bodies that provided ITIL exams. With the contracting of APMG by OGC, the responsibility for ITIL exams is now with APMG. To support the world-wide delivery of these ITIL exams, APMG has accredited a number of exam bodies: EXIN, BCS/ISEB, and Loyalist College, Canada.

1.4   Structure of the book

Chapter 2, introduces the Service Lifecycle, in the context of IT service management and IT governance. It discusses principles of organizational maturity, and the benefits and risks of following a service management framework. This chapter ends with the introduction of the Service Lifecycle.

In Chapters 3 the Continual Service Improvement lifecycle phase is discussed in detail, in a standardized structure.

Chapter 4 provides general information on principles of processes, teams, roles, functions, positions, tools, and other elements of interest.

In chapter 5, the processes and functions of Continual Service Improvement are described in detail. Each of these processes and functions is described in terms of:
- Introduction
- Activities, methods and techniques
- Interfaces, inputs and outputs
- Metrics and Key Performance Indicators (KPIs)
- Implementation, with Critical Success Factors (CSFs), challenges, risks and traps

The appendices provide useful sources for the reader. A reference list of used sources is provided, as well as the official ITIL Glossary and a list with acronyms. The book ends with an extensive index of relevant terms that will support the reader in finding relevant text elements.

CHAPTER 2

Introduction to the Service Lifecycle

2.1 Introduction to ITIL

In the 1980s the quality of service provided by both internal and external IT companies to UK government departments was of such a level that the CCTA (Central Computer and Telecommunications Agency, now the Office of Government Commerce, OGC) was instructed by the Government to develop a standard approach for an efficient and effective delivery of IT services. This was to be an approach which was independent of the suppliers (whether internal or external). The result of this instruction was the development and publication of the **Information Technology Infrastructure Library™** (ITIL). ITIL is made up of a collection of "best practices " found across the range of IT service providers.

ITIL offers a systematic approach to the delivery of quality of IT services. It gives a detailed description of most of the important processes in an IT organization, and includes checklists for tasks, procedures and responsibilities which can be used as a basis for tailoring to the needs of individual organizations.

At the same time, the broad coverage of ITIL also provides a helpful reference guide for many areas, which can be used to develop new improvement goals for an IT organization, enabling it to grow and mature.

Over the years, ITIL has become much more than a series of useful books about IT service management. The framework for the "best practice" in IT service management is promoted and further developed by advisors, trainers and suppliers of technologies or products. Since the nineties, ITIL represents not only the theoretical framework, but the approach and philosophy shared by the people who work with it in practice.

Being an extended framework of best practices for IT service management itself, the advantages and disadvantages of frameworks in general, described in Section 2.5, are also applicable to ITIL. Of course, ITIL was developed because of the advantages mentioned earlier. Many of the pointers from "best practices" are intended to avoid potential problems, or, should they occur after all, to solve them.

ITIL exams

In 2007 the APM Group launched a new certification scheme for ITIL, based on ITIL version 3. ITIL version 2 will be maintained for a transition period, continuing until the year 2008. **ITIL version 2** has qualifications on three levels:
- **Foundation** Certificate in IT Service Management
- **Practitioner** Certificate in IT Service Management
- **Manager** Certificate in IT Service Management

Until 2000, some 60,000 ITIL certificates had been distributed and by 2006 the number had reached 500,000 certificates.

For **ITIL version 3** a new system of qualifications has been set up. There are four qualification levels:
- Foundation Level
- Intermediate Level (Lifecycle Stream & Capability Stream)
- ITIL Diploma
- Advanced Service Management Professional Diploma

For more information about the ITIL V3 Qualification Scheme, see http://www.itil-officialsite.com/Qualifications/ITILV3QualificationScheme.asp.

2.2 IT governance

With the growing role of information, information systems and IT service management, the management requirements for IT grew as well. These requirements focus on two aspects: the compliance with internal and external policies, laws and regulations, and the provision of added value to the stakeholders of the organization. IT governance is still a very young discipline, with no more than a few acknowledged standards or frameworks available. In contrast, there are many different definitions of IT governance available. A definition that receives a lot of support is the one by Van Grembergen:

> *IT governance* consists of a comprehensive framework of structures, processes and relational mechanisms. Structures involve the existence of responsible functions such as IT executives and accounts, and a diversity of IT Committees. Processes refer to strategic IT decision-making and monitoring. Relational mechanisms include business/IT participation and partnerships, strategic dialogue and shared learning.

There is a clear distinction between governance and management, suggesting that governance enables the creation of a setting in which others can manage their tasks effectively (Sohal & Fitzpatrick). So IT governance and IT management are two separate entities. IT service management can be considered to be part of the IT management domain, which leaves IT governance in the business or information management domain.

Although many frameworks are characterized as "IT Governance frameworks", such as CoBiT and even ITIL, most of them are in fact management frameworks. There is at least one standard for IT Governance available: the local Australian standard for Corporate governance of information and communication technology (AS8015-2005).

2.3 Organizational maturity

From the moment **Richard Nolan** introduced his "staged model" for the application of IT in organizations in 1973, many people have used stepwise improvement models. These models were quickly recognized as suitable instruments for quality improvement programs, thereby helping organizations to climb up the maturity ladder.

Dozens of variations on the theme can easily be found, ranging from trades such as software development, acquisition, systems engineering, software testing, website development, data warehousing and security engineering, to help desks and knowledge management. Obviously the *kaizen* principle (improvement works best in smaller steps) was one that appealed to many.

After Nolan's staged model in 1973, the most appealing application of this modeling was found when the Software Engineering Institute (SEI) of Carnegie Mellon University, USA, published its Software Capability Maturity Model (SW-CMM). The CMM was copied and applied in most of the cases mentioned above, making CMM something of a standard in maturity modeling. The CMM was later followed by newer editions, including CMMI (CMM Integration).

Later, these models were applied in quality management models, like the European Foundation for Quality Management (EFQM). Apart from the broad quality management models, there are several other industry accepted practices, such as Six Sigma and Total Quality Management (TQM) which are complementary to ITIL.

The available standards, and frameworks of best practice, offer guidance for organizations in achieving "operational excellence" in IT service management. Depending upon their stage of development, organizations tend to require different kinds of guidance.

Maturity model: CMMI

In the IT industry, the process maturity improvement process is best known in the context of the **Capability Maturity Model Integration (CMMI)**. This process improvement method was developed by the Software Engineering Institute (SEI) of Carnegie Mellon University. CMMI provides both a staged and a continuous model. In the continuous representation, improvement is measured using capability levels. Maturity is measured for a particular process across an organization. In the staged representation, improvement is measured using maturity levels, for a set of processes across an organization.

The capability levels in the **CMMI continuous representation** are:

- **incomplete process** - a process that either is not performed or partially performed
- **performed process** - satisfies the specific goals of the process area
- **managed process** - a performed (capability level 1) process that has the basic infrastructure in place to support the process
- **defined process** - a managed (capability level 2) process that is tailored from the organization's set of standard processes according to the organization's tailoring guidelines, and contributes work products, measures and other process improvement information to the organizational process assets
- **quantitatively Managed process** - a defined (capability level 3) process that is controlled using statistical and other quantitative techniques
- **optimizing process** - a quantitatively managed (capability level 4) process that is improved based on an understanding of the common causes of variation inherent in the process

The **CMMI staged representation** model defines five maturity levels, each a layer in the base for the next phase in the ongoing process improvement, designated by the numbers 1 through 5:

1. **initial** - processes are ad hoc and chaotic
2. **managed** - the projects of the organization have ensured that processes are planned and executed in accordance with policy
3. **defined** - processes are well characterized and understood, and are described in standards, procedures, tools and methods

4. **quantitatively managed** - the organization and projects establish quantitative objectives for quality and process performance, and use them as criteria in managing processes
5. **optimizing** - focuses on continually improving process performance through incremental and innovative process and technological improvements

Many other maturity models were based on these structures, such as the Gartner Maturity Models. Most of these models are focused at capability maturity. Some others, like KPMG's World Class IT Maturity Model, take a different approach.

Standard: ISO/IEC 20000

Developing and maintaining a quality system which complies with the requirements of the ISO 9000 (ISO-9000:2000) series can be considered a tool for the organization to reach and maintain the system-focused (or "managed" in IT Service CMM) level of maturity. These ISO standards emphasize the definition, description and design of processes. For IT service management organizations, a specific ISO standard was produced: the ISO/IEC 20000 (see Figure 2.1).

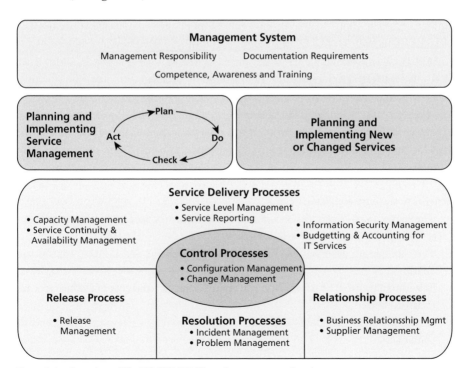

Figure 2.1   Overview of the ISO/IEC 20000 service management system

Customer maturity

When assessing the maturity of an organization, we cannot restrict ourselves to the service provider. The **level of maturity of the customer** (Figure 2.2) is also important. If there are large differences in maturity between the provider and the customer, then these will have to be considered to prevent a mismatch in the approach, methods and mutual expectations. Specifically, this affects the communication between the customer and the provider.

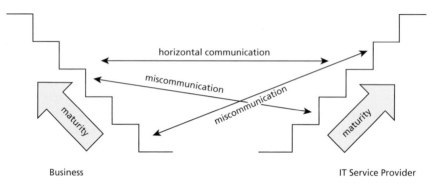

Figure 2.2 Communication and maturity levels: customer and provider

2.4   Benefits and risks of ITSM frameworks

The list below identifies some benefits and possible problems of using IT service management best practices. This list is not intended to be definitive, but is provided here as a basis for considering some of the benefits that can be achieved and some of the mistakes that can be made when using common process-based IT service management frameworks:

Benefits to the customer/user:

- The provision of IT services becomes more customer-focused and agreements about service quality improve the relationship.
- The services are described better, in customer language, and in more appropriate detail.
- Better management of the quality, availability, reliability and cost of the services are managed better.
- Communication with the IT organization is improved by agreeing on the points of contact.

Benefits to the IT organization:
- The IT organization develops a clearer structure, becomes more efficient, and is more focused on the corporate objectives.
- The IT organization is more in control of the infrastructure and services it has responsibility for, and changes become easier to manage.
- An effective process structure provides a framework for the effective outsourcing of elements of the IT services.
- Following best practices encourages a cultural change towards providing service, and supports the introduction of quality management systems based on the ISO 9000 series or on ISO/IEC 20000.
- Frameworks can provide coherent frames of reference for internal communication and communication with suppliers, and for the standardization and identification of procedures.

Potential problems/mistakes:
- The introduction can take a long time and require significant effort, and may require a change of culture in the organization; an overambitious introduction can lead to frustration because the objectives are never met.
- If process structures become an objective in themselves, the service quality may be adversely affected; in this scenario, unnecessary or over-engineered procedures are seen as bureaucratic obstacles, which are to be avoided where possible.
- There is no improvement in IT services due a fundamental lack of understanding about what the relevant processes should provide, what the appropriate performance indicators are, and how processes can be controlled.
- Improvement in the provision of services and cost reductions are insufficiently visible, because no baseline data was available for comparison and/or the wrong targets were identified.
- A successful implementation requires the involvement and commitment of personnel at all levels in the organization; leaving the development of the process structures to a specialist department may isolate that department in the organization and it may set a direction that is not accepted by other departments.
- If there is insufficient investment in appropriate training and support tools, justice will not be done to the processes and the service will not be improved; additional resources and personnel may be needed in the short term if the organization is already overloaded by routine IT service management activities which may not be using "best practices".

2.5   Service Lifecycle: concept and overview

The information provision role and system has grown and changed since the launch of ITIL version 2 (in 2000/02). IT supports and is part of an increasing number of goods and services. In the business world, the information provision role has changed as well: IT's role is no longer just supporting, but has become the baseline for the creation of business value.

ITIL version 3 intends to include and provide insight into IT's new role in all its complexity and dynamics. To that end, a new service management approach has been chosen that does not center around processes, but focuses on the Service Lifecycle.

Basic concepts

Before we describe the Service Lifecycle, we need to define some basic concepts.

Good practice

ITIL is presented as a good practice (literally: correct method). This is an approach or method that has proven itself in practice. These good practices can be a solid backing for organizations that want to improve their IT services. In such cases, the best thing to do is to select a generic standard or method that is accessible to everyone, ITIL, COBIT, CMMI, PRINCE2® and ISO/IEC 20000, for example. One of the benefits of these freely accessible generic standards is that they can be applied to several real-life environments and situations. There is also ample training available for open standards. This makes it much easier to train staff.

Another source for good practice is proprietary knowledge. A disadvantage of this kind of knowledge is that it may be customized for the context and needs of a specific organization. Therefore, it may be difficult to adopt or replicate and it may not be as effective in use.

Service

A service is about creating value for the customer. ITIL defines a service as follows:

> A **service** is a means of delivering value to customers by facilitating outcomes the customers want to achieve without the ownership of specific costs or risks.

Outcomes are possible from the performance of tasks, and they are limited by a number of constraints. Services enhance performance and reduce the pressure of constraints. This increases the chances of the desired outcomes being realized.

Value

Value is the core of the service concept. From the customer's perspective value consists of two core components: utility and warranty. Utility is what the customer receives, and warranty is how it is provided.

Service management

ITIL defines service management as follows:

> **Service management** is a set of specialized organizational capabilities for providing value to customers in the form of services.

ITIL discusses some of the fundamental principles of service management that supplement the functions and processes in the ITIL core books. The next principles may help design a service management system:

- **Specialization & coordination** - The goal of service management is to make capabilities and resources available through services that are useful and acceptable to the customer with regard to quality, costs and risks. The service provider takes the weight of responsibility and resource management off the customer's shoulders so that they can focus on the business' core competence. Service management coordinates the business of service management responsibility with regard to certain resources. *Utility* and *warranty* act as a guide.
- **Agency principle** - Service management always involves an agent and a principal that seconds this agent to fulfill activities on their behalf. Agents may be consultants, advisors or service providers. Service agents act as intermediary between service providers and customers in conjunction with users. Usually, these agents are the service provider's staff, but they can also be self-service systems and processes for users. Value for the customer is created through agreements between principals and agents.
- **Encapsulation** - The customer's interest focuses on the value of use; he prefers to be spared from any technical details and structure complexity. The "encapsulation principle" is focused on hiding what the customer does not need and showing what is valuable and useful to the customer. Three principles are closely linked to this:
  - separation of concerns
  - modularity: a clear, modular structure
  - loose coupling: reciprocal independence of resources and users

Systems
ITIL describes the organizational structure concepts which proceed from system theory. The Service Lifecycle in ITIL version 3 is a system; however, a function, a process or an organization is a system as well. The definition of a system:

> A **system** is a group of interacting, interrelating, or interdependent components that form a unified whole, operating together for a common purpose.

Feedback and learning are two key aspects in the performance of systems; they turn processes, functions and organizations into dynamic systems. Feedback can lead to learning and growth, not only within a process, but also within an organization in its entirety.

Within a process, for instance, the feedback about the performance of one cycle is, in its turn, input for the next process cycle. Within organizations, there can be feedback between processes, functions and lifecycle phases. Behind this feedback is the common goal: the customer's objectives.

Functions and processes
The distinction between functions and processes is important in ITIL.

What is a function?

> A **function** is a subdivision of an organization that is specialized in fulfilling a specified type of work, and is responsible for specific end results.
> Functions are independent subdivisions with capabilities and resources that are required for their performance and results. They have their own practices and their own knowledge body.

What is a process?

> A **process** is a structured set of activities designed to accomplish a defined objective.
> Processes result in a goal-oriented change, and utilize feedback for self-enhancing and self-corrective actions.

Processes possess the following characteristics:
- They are **measurable** because they are performance-oriented.
- They have **specific results**.
- They provide results to **customers** or stakeholders.
- They **respond to a specific event** - a process is indeed continual and iterative, but is always originating from a certain event.

It can be difficult to determine whether something is a function or a process. According to ITIL, whether it is a function or process depends completely on the organizational design. A good example of a function is a service desk, a good example of a process is change management.

The hierarchical structure of functions can lead to the rise of "silos" in which each function is very self-oriented. This does not benefit the success of the organization as a whole. Processes run through the hierarchical structure of functions; functions often share some processes. This is how processes suppress the rise of functional silos, and help to ensure an improved coordination in between functions.

The Service Lifecycle

ITIL version 3 approaches service management from the lifecycle of a service. The Service Lifecycle is an organization model providing insight into:
- the way service management is structured
- the way the various lifecycle components are linked to each other
- the impact that changes in one component will have on other components and on the entire lifecycle system

So the new ITIL version focuses on the Service Lifecycle, and the way service management components are linked. The processes are also discussed (both the old familiar ones and the new ones) in the cycle phases. They describe how things change.

The Service Lifecycle consists of five phases. Each volume of the new ITIL books describes one of these phases:
- **Service Strategy** - the phase of designing, developing and implementing service management as a strategic resource
- **Service Design** - the design phase of developing appropriate IT services, including architecture, processes, policy and documents; the design goal is to meet the current and future business requirements
- **Service Transition** - the phase of developing and improving capabilities for the transition of new and modified services to production

- **Service Operation** - the phase of achieving effectiveness and efficiency in providing and supporting services in order to ensure value for the customer and the service provider
- **Continual Service Improvement** - the phase of creating and maintaining the value for the customer by design improvement, and service introduction and operation

Service Strategy is the axis of the Service Lifecycle (Figure 2.3) that "runs" all other phases; it is the phase of policymaking and objectives. The phases Service Design, Service Transition and Service Operation implement this strategy, their continual theme is adjustment and change. The Continual Service Improvement phase stands for learning and improving, and embraces all cycle phases. This phase initiates improvement programs and projects, and prioritizes them based on the strategic objectives of the organization.

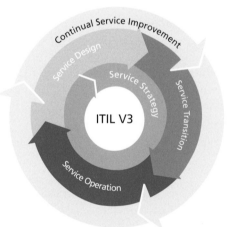

Figure 2.3 The Service Lifecycle

The Service Lifecycle is a combination of many perspectives on the reality of organizations. This offers more flexibility and control.

The dominant pattern in the Service Lifecycle is the succession of Service Strategy to Service Design, to Service Transition and to Service Operation, and then, through Continual Service Improvement, back to Service Strategy, and so on. The cycle encompasses, however, many patterns. Depending on tasks and responsibilities, a manager can choose his own control perspective. If you are responsible for the design, development or improvement of processes, the best perspective to use is a process perspective. If you are responsible for managing SLAs, contracts and services, the Service Lifecycle perspective and its various phases is likely to meet your needs better.

ITIL Library

The official, new style ITIL Library encompasses the following components:
- Core Library - the five Service Lifecycle publications:
  - Service Strategy
  - Service Design
  - Service Transition
  - Service Operation
  - Continual Service Improvement

  Each book covers a phase from the Service Lifecycle and encompasses various processes. The processes are always described in detail in the book in which they find their key application.
- Complementary portfolio:
  - introduction guide
  - key element guides
  - qualification aids
  - white papers
  - glossary

CHAPTER 3

Lifecycle Phase: Continual Service Improvement

3.1 Introduction

IT must continually align and re-align IT services to the changing business needs by identifying and implementing improvements to IT services that support the business. ITIL version 3 places this within the lifecycle phase of **Continual Service Improvement**.

In English there is a difference between *continual* and *continuous*:

*   *continuous* means that the organization is involved in an activity without interruption; the efforts are constantly at the same level; for example, *continuous operation*
*   *continual* means a succession of closely placed activities; in this way a sequence of improvement efforts is created: *continual improvement*

An IT service is created by a number of activities. The quality of these activities and the process which links these activities determine the quality of the eventual service. CSI focuses on the activities and processes to improve the quality of services. To this end, it uses the *Plan-Do-Check-Act* Cycle of Deming (PDCA). This cycle prescribes a consolidation phase for each improvement, to engrain the new procedures in the organization. This implies a repeating pattern of improvement efforts with varying levels of intensity, instead of a single continuing improvement effort which is always on the same level. This is the reason why, in ITIL version 3, the "C" of CSI stands for continual and not continuous.

Measuring and analyzing is crucial to CSI; by measuring it is possible to identify which services are profitable and which services can do better. The **CSI improvement process** has a seven step plan. Creating a **Service Improvement Plan (SIP)** is an SLM activity within the CSI scope. The Section "Processes and other activities" pursues this matter in more depth. Next we will describe the roles which execute the core activities, followed by the methods, techniques and technology which assist them. The interfaces between service level management and CSI are dealt with in the last section on interfaces with the other phases and IT service management processes from the ITIL lifecycle. First of all, we will consider the justification of CSI and a number of basic concepts.

Goal and objectives

The **goal** of CSI is for continual improvement of the effectiveness and efficiency of IT services, allowing them to meet the business requirements better. This entails both achieving and surpassing the objectives (**effectiveness**), and obtaining these objectives at the lowest cost possible (**efficiency**). To increase the effectiveness you can, for instance, reduce the number of errors in a process. To make a process more efficient you can eliminate unnecessary activities or automate manual operations.

By measuring and analyzing the process results in all Service Lifecycle phases you can determine which results are structurally worse than others. These offer the highest improvement probability.

CSI mainly measures and monitors the following matters:
- **Process compliance** - Does the organization follow the new or modified service management processes and does it use the new tools?
- **Quality** - Do the various process activities meet their goals?
- **Performance** - How efficient is the process? What are the elapsed times?
- **Business value of a process** - Does the process make a difference? Is it effective? How does the client rate the process?

The main **objectives** of CSI are:
- to measure and analyze **service level achievements** by comparing them to the requirements in the Service Level Agreement (SLA)
- to recommend improvements in all phases of the lifecycle
- to introduce activities which will increase the quality, efficiency, effectiveness and customer satisfaction of the services and the IT service management processes
- to operate more cost effective IT services without sacrificing customer satisfaction
- to use suitable quality management methods for improvement activities

Scope

The scope of CSI contains three important areas:
- general quality of the IT management
- continual tuning of the IT services to the current and future needs of the business
- continual tuning of the IT service portfolio
- the maturity of the IT processes which make the services possible

3.2 Basic concepts

CSI and Organizational Change

In order to make continual improvement a permanent part of the organizational culture, a change in mentality is often needed. This is one of the most difficult aspects of CSI and, in reality, a lot of CSI programs fail because they do not (or cannot) achieve this cultural change. John P. Kotter, *Professor of Leadership* at the Harvard Business School, examined over a hundred companies and discovered eight crucial steps needed to successfully change an organization:
- **create a sense of urgency** - for instance, answer the question "what if we do nothing?"
- **form a leading coalition** - a single pioneer cannot change an entire organization; a small key team is needed with the necessary authority and resources; this team can be expanded as the support grows
- **create a vision** - a good vision formulates the goal and the purpose of CSI, provides direction, motivates, coordinates and formulates goals for the senior management; make these goals SMART: *Specific, Measurable, Achievable/Appropriate, Realistic/ Relevant* and *Timely/Time-bound*; without a vision, a CSI program will soon become a repository of projects which do not have obvious benefits for the organization; tailor the vision to the client's requirements
- **communicate the vision** - each stakeholder must know what the vision is, what is its use for them, and why CSI is needed; to achieve this, put together a communication plan, and demonstrate by example
- **empower others to act on the vision** - remove obstacles, give direction by setting clear goals and supply people with the proper resources such as tools and training; create security and self confidence; only then will they be able to take responsibility for their part in CSI
- **plan for and create quick wins** - evaluate per service or process what can be improved rapidly; plan this, execute it and communicate it in order to increase support

- **consolidate improvements and create more change** - quick wins convince and motivate; medium term successes offer confidence in the organization's own improvement capabilities and foresee a set of standard procedures; but in the long run improvement can only be considered a success if people and processes are continually improving themselves
- **institutionalize the changes**:
  - hire personnel with experience in best practices in the field of IT management
  - from day one hand out work instructions
  - clarify what the procedures are
  - train staff in IT management
  - match the goals and reports to changing demands
  - define clear action points in the minutes
  - integrate new IT solutions and development projects in existing processes

Combined with good project management, these steps will considerably increase the chances of success.

The PDCA Cycle

A *"big bang"* approach does not usually result in a successful improvement program. That is why the American statistician Dr W Edwards Deming developed a step-by-step improvement approach in the 1980s: the ***Plan-Do-Check-Act* Cycle** (**PDCA**):
- **Plan** - what needs to happen, who will do what and how?
- **Do** - execute the planned activities
- **Check** - check whether the activities yield the desired result
- **Act** - adjust the plan in accordance to the checks

Next is a consolidation phase to engrain the changes into the organization. The Cycle is also known as the **Deming Cycle** (Figure 3.1).

CSI uses the PDCA Cycle in two areas:
- implementation of CSI
- continual improvement of services and processes

First, we discuss the Cycle for the *implementation of CSI* (Figure 3.2):
- **plan CSI**:
  - determine the scope
  - determine the requirements CSI must meet
  - set goals, for instance using gap analysis
  - define action points

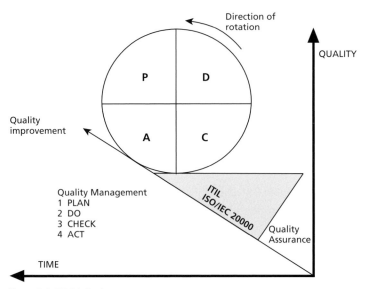

Figure 3.1 PDCA Cycle

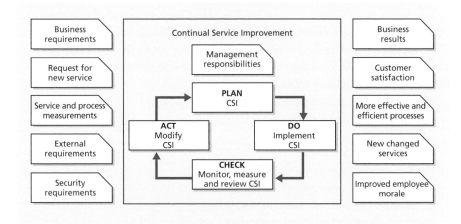

Figure 3.2 PDCA Cycle for the improvement of services, applied to the introduction of CSI (in accordance to ISO/IEC 20000)

- determine which checks need to be executed during the check phase
- determine the interfaces between CSI and the rest of the lifecycle
- determine which process activities need to be introduced
- set (management) roles and responsibilities
- find out which tools are needed to support and document processes

- select the methods and techniques to measure and document the quality and effectiveness of the services and processes
- **implement CSI (*do*):**
  - determine the budget
  - document roles and responsibilities
  - determine the CSI policy, plans and procedures, maintain these, communicate about them and train your staff
  - supply monitoring, analysis and reporting tools
  - integrate CSI with Service Strategy, Service Design, Service Transition and Service Operation
- **monitor, measure and evaluate CSI (*check*):**
  - report on the accomplishments with regard to the plans
  - evaluate the documentation
  - perform process assessments and audits
  - formulate proposals for process improvement
- **adjust CSI (*act*):**
  - introduce the improvements
  - adjust the policy, procedures, roles and responsibilities

During the implementation of CSI all phases play an important part. In the second area where the PDCA Cycle is used - *continual improvement of services and processes* - the focus is mainly on the "check" and "act" phase. There are, however, also activities in the "plan" and "do" phase which are involved:

- **plan improvement initiatives**:
  - set goals and check methods
  - perform gap analysis
  - determine action points
- **implement the improvement initiative**:
  - eliminate the discrepancies found
  - provide a smooth execution of the process
- **monitor, check and evaluate services and processes**:
  - compare the checks after the improvement to those prior to the improvement and to the goals set in the plan phase
  - determine whether the discrepancies found need to be eliminated
  - make recommendations for the improvement such as adjusting the service catalogue and the new SLA checks
- **continual improvement of services and processes**:
  - introduce the improvements

- determine which discrepancies need to be addressed, this constitutes the input for the plan phase

Metrics, KPIs and CSFs

An IT service manager needs to know whether their organization as a whole meets its goals and which processes contribute to this. A **metric** measures the results of a process or activity by determining whether a certain variable meets its set target. For instance, a metric measures whether the required number of incidents are resolved within one hour.

Metrics are mainly interpreted on a strategic and tactical level. They must describe all processes within an organization. Three types are needed for CSI:

- **technology metrics** - measure the performance and availability of components and applications
- **process metrics** - measure the performance of service management processes; they stem from **Key Performance Indicators** (**KPIs**), which in turn stem from **Critical Success Factors** (CSFs); also see step four of the CSI improvement process: "process data"; these metrics help to determine the improvement opportunities for each process
- **service metrics** - the results of the end service; these are measured using component metrics

A metric stems from the goal set by an organization. If the business views IT as a *cost center* then it will probably want to decrease the costs. If, however, it sees IT as the enabler of the company, then the goal will probably be to develop flexible services which will decrease the *time-to-market*. The measuring system should not focus solely on only one of the three aspects of money, time and quality, otherwise the remaining two aspects will receive insufficient attention.

For the business mission, **CSFs** are defined: these are elements essential to achieving the mission. The **KPIs** following on from these CSFs determine the quality, performance, value and process compliance. They can either be *qualitative* (such as customer satisfaction), or *quantitative* (such as costs of a printer incident).

At the start of the improvement program two to three KPIs per CSF will already supply a great deal of information which will need to be processed. The KPIs can be extended or adjusted later according to new developments. For instance, if the organization has achieved its goals or when new service management processes are introduced.

Determine if the KPI is suitable by answering these questions:
- Do we achieve our goals if we achieve the KPI?
- Can the KPI be interpreted correctly? Does it help in determining the action needed?
- Who needs the information? When? How often? How fast does the information need to be available?
- Is the KPI stable and accurate or subject to external, uncontrollable influences?
- How easy is it to adjust the KPI to new developments?
- To what extent can the KPI be measured now? Under what circumstances?
- Who collects and analyzes the measurements? Who is responsible for the improvements resulting from this information?

Data, information, knowledge and wisdom (DIKW)

Metrics supply quantitative **data**; for instance, that the service desk registers 12,000 incidents each month. CSI transforms this data into qualitative **information**, a received and understood message which stems from processed and grouped data; such as the fact that 18% of the incidents reported are related to the organization's email facility. By combining information with experience, context, interpretation and reflection it becomes **knowledge**; for example, since we know that the organization is a web store, we can determine the impact of the incidents concerning the email facility.

What it comes down to in CSI is **wisdom**: being able to make the correct assessments and the correct decisions by using the data, information and knowledge in the best possible way. For example, because we know the impact of the email incidents on the client, we can decide to focus on this service because we want to improve our customer service. The CSI improvement process focuses on the acquirement of wisdom (see the Section "Processes and other activities" and step 6 in the CSI improvement process about service reporting).

Governance

Governance drives organizations and controls them. *Corporate governance* provides a good, honest, transparent and responsible management of an organization. *Business governance* results in good company performances. Together they are known as *enterprise governance*.

IT governance is also part of *enterprise governance*. It shapes the processes and structure of an IT organization and ensures that it achieves its goals. Complying with the new rules, such as the American *Sarbanes-Oxley Act* from 2002 (corporate governance), and constantly performing better at a lower cost (business governance) are both part of IT governance.

These two developments are the main motive for CSI: IT service providers must offer their services from a strategic rather than a tactical perspective. IT departments which only focus on technology will soon become less appealing to their business.

An ITSM standard such as ITIL helps to control an organization by forging it into a coherent system of roles, responsibilities, processes, policy and *controls*.

CSI policies and procedures
CSI policies capture agreements about measuring, reporting, service levels, CSFs, KPIs and evaluations. These must be known to the whole organization. Most organizations assess the process results each month. It is wise to evaluate new services more often.

An IT organization should implement the following CSI policies:
- all improvement initiatives must go through the change management process
- all functional groups are responsible for CSI activities
- CSI roles and responsibilities are recorded and announced (see Section "Organization")

3.3 Processes and other activities
To improve the services of the IT organization CSI measures the yield of these services. The main CSI activities are:
- **check**:
  - check the results of the processes
  - examine customer satisfaction
  - assess process maturity
  - check whether the staff follow the internal guidelines
  - analyze the measurement data and compare these to the goals set in the SLA
- **report**:
  - propose improvements for all phases in the lifecycle
  - consider the relevance of existing goals
- **improve**:
  - introduce activities which increase the quality, efficiency, effectiveness and customer satisfaction of the services
  - use appropriate quality management methods for improvement activities

Setting directions

The effect of the improvement is greatly determined by the direction in which the improvement takes place.

> "Would you tell me, please, which way I ought to go from here?"
>
> "That depends a good deal on where you want to get to," said the Cat.
>
> "I don't much care where -" said Alice.
>
> "Then it doesn't matter which way you go," said the Cat.
>
> "- so long as I get somewhere," Alice added as an explanation.
>
> "Oh, you're sure to do that," said the Cat, "if you only walk long enough."
>
> Source: Lewis Carroll, Alice's Adventures in Wonderland, 1865

Without a vision a bout the direction of the improvement, an improvement has only a limited value. Because of this, determine a vision including its goals before you start with an improvement process.

The organization must continually assess its current improvement course (CSI goals) on relevance, completeness and feasibility. The **CSI model** in Figure 3.3 can provide some support.

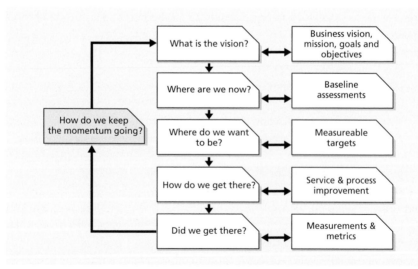

Figure 3.3 CSI model

This continual cycle consists of six phases:

1. **Determine the vision** - IT gets an insight into the goals of its business, and together with the business formulates a vision to tune the IT strategy to the business strategy; together they formulate a mission, goals and objectives.
2. **Record the current situation** - Record the starting point (baseline) of the client, organization, people, process and technology.
3. **Determine measurable targets** - Set priorities together with the client based on the vision: what do we improve first, how extensive must the improvement be and when should it be finished?
4. **Plan** - Draw up a detailed service improvement plan (SIP) including actions to achieve the desired situation.
5. **Check** - Measure whether the objectives have been achieved, and check whether the processes are complied with.
6. **Assure** - Engrain the changes in order to maintain them.

Announce this plan to the whole organization in order to create a consciousness, understanding, enthusiasm and support. Create a dialogue with the organization and regularly communicate and report on the actual achievements.

Service measurement

In order to determine the current situation, step two of the CSI model must measure an organization. This means that they must be able to determine the value of their services with regard to the service levels which have been agreed upon. They must also be able to report on this to their client. This requires that the organization knows which components, systems and applications are responsible for which part of the service.

By measuring an organization can also prove when the client itself is responsible for a failure. As a result the client can increase its knowledge level through training.

The section on the CSI improvement process in Chapter 5 goes deeper into the subject of service measurement.

The CSI improvement process

The **CSI improvement process** or 7-step improvement process describes how you should measure and report. The plan phase in CSI yields a **Service Improvement Plan (SIP)**.

If service level management discovers that something can be improved, it will pass this on to CSI. CSI can then formulate activities which will bring about the improvement.

For the execution CSI generates a SIP. This turns "improvement" into an IT process with input, activities, output, roles and reporting.

CSI measures and processes these measurements in a continual improvement process. This goes **from measuring to improving in seven steps**:

1. what *should* you measure?
2. What *can* you measure?
3. Gather data (measure).
4. Process data.
5. Analyze data.
6. Present and use the information.
7. Implement corrective action.

Chapter 5 contains an elaborate section on the CSI improvement process.

Service reporting
Service reporting is the process which is responsible for the generation and supply of reports about the results achieved and the developments in service levels. An extensive description of the service reporting process can be found in Chapter 5.

3.4 Organization
Process activities are not limited to one part of the organization. Because of this the process manager must map the defined process roles and activities to existing staff. Clear definitions of the responsibility and accountability are required, for instance in a **RACI matrix** (*Responsible, Accountable, Consulted, Informed*).

Roles and responsibilities
CSI comprises permanent production roles such as **service manager, service owner, process owner** and analysts, and temporary project roles such as project managers and project team members.

Table 3.1 provides an overview of the accompanying key activities and roles. Not all roles are full-time. Make a global division and adjust this later on if needed.

Key activity	Key role
Gether data from the measurement of service results and service management processes and compare these to the starting point (baseline), goals SLAs and benchmarks: analyze trends	Service manager, service owner, IT process owner
Set targets for efficiency improvement and cost effectiveness throughout the entire Service Lifecycle	Service manager
Set targets for service improvements and use of resources	Service manager, service owner, business process owner
Consider new business and security requirements	Service manager, business process owner
Create on SIP and implement improvements	Service manager, service owner, process owner
Enable personnel to propose improvements	Service manager
Measure, report and communicate about improvement initiatives	Service manager
Revise policy, processes procedures and plans if needed	Service manager
Ensure that all approved actions are completed and that they achieve the desired result	Service manager, business manager, IT process owner, business process owner

Table 3.1 Key activities and the roles to be divided

Table 3.2 provides an overview of the roles, activities and skills needed for the different steps in the CSI improvement process.

Step	Roles	Activity types	Skills
1. What should you measure?	Decision makers, such as the **service manager, service owner, service level manager, CSI manager, process owner**	• high management level • high variation • action oriented • communicative • focues on future	• management skills • communicate • create and use conceptes • handle complex and uncertain situations • education and experience
2. What can you measure?	Internal and external service providers who know the possibilities, such as the service manager, **service owner, process owner** and the process manager	• intellectual • investigative • medium to high variation • goal oriented • speciallzed in business management	• analyze • model • inventive attitude • education • program

Step	Roles	Activity types	Skills
3. Gether data (measure)	Personnel who supply services in the Service Transition and Service Operation life phases, such as the service desk personnel on a daily basis	• standardlized • routine (low variation) • automated • clerical level • procedural	• accuracy • precision • applied training • technical experience
4. Process data	See step 3	• specialized • structures • automated • medium variation • procedural	• numerical skills • methodical • accurate • applied training • programming • experience with tools
5. Analyze data	Internal and external service providers who know the possibilities, such as the **service owner, process owner** and the business and IT analysts	See step 2	See step 2
6. Present and use the information (reporting)	Internal and external service providers who know the possibilities and the main decision makers, such as the **CSI manager, service manager, service owner, service level manager, process owner**	See step 1	See step 1
7. Implement corrective actions	See step 6	See step 2	See step 2

Table 3.2 Roles for the CSI improvement process

For the ITIL Foundations exam, knowledge is required on the roles printed in bold in Table 3.2. We will discuss these further, except for the role of **service level manager**.

Figure 3.4 shows how the various roles can cooperate.

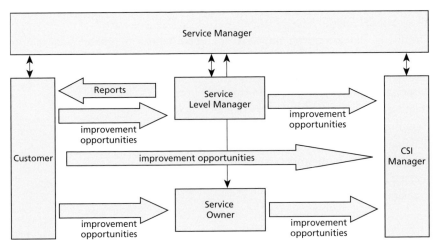

Figure 3.4 How the various roles cooperate effectively

Service manager

The **service manager** manages the development, implementation, evaluation and ongoing management of new and existing products and services. The service manager is responsible for:

- achieving company strategy and goals
- benchmarking
- financial management
- customer management
- vendor management
- full lifecycle management
- inventory management

The service manager must know a great deal about market analysis, be able to anticipate new market needs, formulate complex programs, guide personnel and sell services.

CSI manager

Without a clear and unambiguous responsibility, improvement will not occur. As a result this new role is essential for a successful improvement program. The **CSI manager** is responsible for CSI in the organization. The CSI manager manages the measuring, analysis, investigating and reporting of trends and initiates service improvement activities. In addition, they also makes sure that sufficient CSI supporting resources are available. They are responsible for:

- development of the CSI domain
- awareness and communication of CSI throughout the organization

- allocating CSI roles
- identifying and prioritzing improvement opportunities to senior management together with the service owner
- identifying monitoring requirements together with the service level manager
- ensuring that the proper monitoring tools are installed
- creating SIPs together with the service level manager
- capturing baseline data to measure improvement against it
- defining and reporting upon CSFs, KPIs and activity metrics
- using supporting frameworks and models
- making knowledge management an integral part of the daily routine
- evaluating analyzed data

The CSI manager must be able to lead projects throughout the organization, build good relationships with the business and IT management, have a flair for improvement opportunities throughout the company and be able to counsel staff.

Service owner

It is crucial to appoint one person responsible for each service: this is the **service owner**. They are the central point of contact for a specific service. It does not matter where the underlying technological components, process or functions are located. The main responsibilities are:

- owning and representing the service
- understanding which components make up the service
- measuring the performance and availability
- attending *Change Advisory Board* (CAB) meetings if these changes are relevant to the service they represent
- working with the CSI manager to identify and prioritize improvements
- participating in internal and external service reviews
- maintaining the service entry in the service catalogue
- participating in the negotiation of SLAs and OLAs

Process owner

Having an owner is just as crucial to a process as a service owner is to a service. The **process owner** ensures that the organization follows a process. They must be a senior manager with enough credibility, influence and authority in the organization departments which are part of the process. The process owner performs the essential role of process champion, design lead, advocate, coach and protector.

Other roles
Other roles which are important to CSI:
- **Service knowledge manager** - designs and maintains a knowledge management strategy and implements this
- **Reporting analyst** - evaluates and analyzes data, and identifies trends; often cooperates with SLM roles; must have good communication skills because reporting is an essential element of communication
- **Communication responsibility** - designs a communication strategy for CSI

3.5 Methods, techniques and tools

There are various methods and techniques to check whether planned improvements actually produce measurable improvements. One method or technique is not usually enough: you need to find the best mix for your organization. Check whether the chosen methods and techniques are suitable to measure the results of your processes, document them thoroughly and instruct staff who will be using the method or technique.

Implementation review

To determine whether the improvements produce the desired effects, you have to ask whether the original problem situation has actually improved, and how the organization has planned and implemented the improvement. The following questions help with this:
- Have we correctly assessed the present situation and have we properly formulated the problem?
- Have we taken the correct decisions with respect to our strategy?
- Have we adopted the strategy in the right way?
- Have we formulated the right CSI goals?
- Have the goals been reached?
- Do we now provide better IT services?
- What are the lessons learned and where are we now?

Assessments

An assessment compares the performance of an operational process against a performance standard. This can be an agreement in an SLA, a maturity standard, or a benchmark of companies in the same industry. By conducting assessments, IT organizations show their commitment to improvement in maturity.

Assessments are very well suited to answer the question "where are we now?", and to determine the extent of the gap with "where we want to be". A well-designed maturity assessment framework evaluates the viability of all aspects of the process environment including the people, process and technology as well as factors effecting overall process effectiveness in the business. Keep in mind that the desired performance or maturity level of a process depends on the impact that the process has on the customer's business processes.

First determine the relationship between business processes, IT services, IT systems and components. CSI can separately assess the effectiveness and efficiency results for each component. This helps in identifying areas for improvement.

It is crucial to clearly define what is being assessed. Base this on the goals and the expected future use of assessment and assessment reports. An assessment can take place on three levels:
- **process only** - only assess process attributes based on the general principles and guidelines of the process framework which defines the subject process
- **people, process and technology** - also assess skills, roles and talents of managers and staff who participate in the process; also assess the process-supporting technology
- **full assessment** - also assess the culture of acceptance within the organization, the ability of the organization to articulate a process strategy, the definition of a vision for the process environment as an "end-state", the structure and function of the process organization, and so on

All these factors are compared to the maturity attributes of the selected maturity model.

Assessments are useful in the:
- **planning phase** - as starting point (baseline) for process performance
- **implementation phase** (*do*) - to check that the estimates are correct
- **measurement phase** (*check*) - to complete the balance and to identify further possible improvements

Advantages of assessments:
- they can measure certain parts of a process independently of the rest and determine the impact of that specific component on the rest of the process
- they can be repeated

Disadvantages of assessments:
- they only offer a snapshot in time and do not give insight into the cultural dynamic of an organization

- they can become a goal in themselves instead of a means to an end
- they are labour intensive
- the results are still dependent on subjective assessors and therefore not entirely objective, even if the measurements are

This applies to both internal and external assessments. Table 3.3 gives an overview of the advantages and disadvantages of both forms.

Internal assessment	
Advantages	**Disadvantages**
• no expensive consultants	• less objective
• self assessment sets are available for free	• disappointing acceptance of findings
• promotes internal co-operation and communication	• internal politice can get involved
• promotes internal level of knowledge	• limited knowledge of skills
• good starting point for CSI	• labour intensive
• internal knowledge of existing environment	
External assessment	
Advantages	**Disadvantages**
• objectiviity	• high costs
• expert ITIL knowledge	• risk as to acceptance
• wide experience with serveral IT organizations	• limited knowledge of existing environments
• analytical skills	• insufficient preparation limits effectiveness
• credibility	
• minimal impact on the provision of services	

Table 3.3 Internal versus external assessment

Benchmarks

A benchmark is a particular type of assessment: organizations compare (parts of) their processes with the performance of the same types of processes that are commonly recognized as "best practice". This can be done in four ways:

- **internal** - against an earlier starting point (baseline)
- **internal** - against another system or department
- **external** - against industry standards
- **external** - directly with similar organizations; this is only useful, however, if there are enough similar organizations in terms of environment, sector and geographical placement

The form you choose depends on the purpose of the benchmark:
- measurements of costs (price) and performance of internal or external service providers
- compare process performance with the existing industry standard
- compare the financial performance of high-level IT costs with industry standard or other organizations
- measure effectiveness in achieving the required customer satisfaction

To determine this you can set up an organizational profile, which consists of four key components:
- **company information profile** - basic information such as scope and type of organization
- **current assets** - hardware such as desktops and servers
- **current best practices** - policy, procedures and tools and the degree to which they are used in the organization
- **complexity** - the number of end users and the quantity and type of technology in your organization

In all cases a benchmark provides the following results:
- represents performance
- shows the gaps
- shows the risk of not closing these gaps
- helps set priorities
- helps in communicating the information well

In this way organizations discover whether their processes are cost effective, whether they meet customer needs and how effective they are in comparison to other organizations. They become aware of the need to improve and the ways they can do so, for example in the areas of economies of scale, efficiency and effectiveness. Management can then act on this. In the ideal case benchmarking forms part of a continual cycle of improvement and is repeated regularly.

Studies into the performance of one's own organization and other departments or organizations takes time. Setting up a benchmark database and visiting other organizations also involves costs.

Benchmarking is done in cooperation with:
- the business
- users or consumers

- internal service providers
- external service providers
- users in "public domain"
- benchmark partners (other organizations who are involved in the comparison)

First look to see if there are any problem areas. Use the steps from the CSI improvement process, supported by (some of) the following techniques:
- informal discussions with the business, staff or suppliers
- focus groups
- market research
- quantitative research
- surveys
- questionnaires
- re-engineering analysis
- process mapping
- quality control variation reports
- financial ratio analysis

Two special forms of benchmarking are:
- **Process maturity comparison** - as opposed to an assessment, this is not a comparison with the maturity model, but the maturity level is compared with that of other organizations; for example, CMMI can be used as a maturity model
- **Total cost of ownership** (TCO™) - the sum of all the costs of the design, the introduction, operation and improvement of services (developed by Gartner); it is often used to compare specific services in one organization with those of another organization

Balanced Scorecard (BSC)
Kaplan and Norton developed the **Balanced Scorecard** (**BSC**) in the 1990s. Define a balanced scorecard for each business unit. Begin carefully: select two to four goals. Then you can extend this as a "waterfall" to the underlying components, such as the service desk. After successful implementation keep measuring regularly.

Gap analysis
This analysis naturally flows on from assessments and benchmarks. Having determined where the organization is now, the gap analysis will determine the size of the gap with where the organization wants to be. In this way light is shed on new opportunities for improvement. The *service gap model* in Figure 3.5 shows possible gaps or discrepancies.

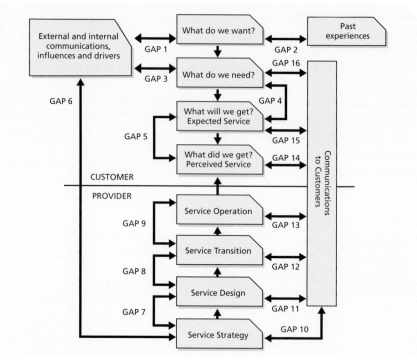

Figure 3.5 Service gap model (after SERVQUAL: Parasuraman, Zeithaml and Berry)

Gap analyses can be the result of a benchmarking on service or process maturity investigations. They can be done on a strategic, tactical or operational level. It gives an overview of the amount of resources and money which an organization has to spend to reach specific goals.

SWOT-analysis

A **SWOT-analysis** looks at the *Strengths, Weaknesses, Opportunities and Threats* of an organization (component) or project. The organization then answers the following questions:

- How can we profit from strong points?
- How can we remove weak points?
- How can we use opportunities optimally?
- How can we manage and eliminate threats?

Set your end goal before you perform a SWOT analysis. Look at which strong points help achieve a goal, which weaknesses prevent you from doing this, what external conditions promote the goal, and what external conditions prevent it.

To arrive at a SWOT of the whole organization, you can first make a SWOT for each organization component or function and then integrate them into a company SWOT. See Table 3.4 for sample aspects of SWOTs.

Possible strenghts	Possible Weaknesses
• core competences	• no clear strategic direction
• financial means	• cutclated facilties
• necognized as a market leader	• low profits
• proven management	• little insight into performance
Possible opportunities	**Possible threats**
• creation of new customer groups	• foreign competition with lower prices
• application of skills and knowledge for new products	• lower market growth
	• expensive legialation and regulation

Table 3.4 Examples of aspects from SWOT analyses

Rummler-Brache swim-lane diagram

Geary Rummler and Alan Brache introduced the idea of representing the relationships between processes and organizations or departments with "swim lanes" in a Rummler-Brache **swim-lane diagram**. This maps the flow of a process: from the customer through the department to the technology (Figure 3.6). The horizontal rows divide the separate organizations or departments from each other. Activities and decisions are connected through arrows to indicate the flow.

The row in which these components are placed indicates which organizational component is responsible for the activity or decision.

Because this instrument places the whole process within a recognizable structure of organizations, it is very useful as a communication tool with the management.

Tools

CSI needs different types of software to support, test, monitor and report on the ITSM processes. As part of the assessment of "where do we want to be?" the requirements for enhancing tools will be addressed and documented. The need and sophistication of

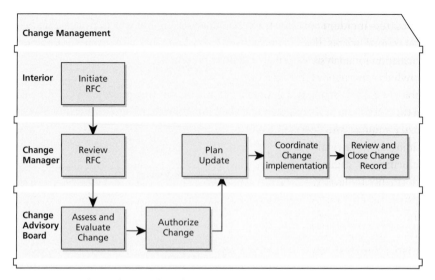

Figure 3.6 Rummler-Brache swim-lane diagram

the tools required depend on the business need for IT services and to some extent the size of the organization.

In any case, tools must monitor and analyze the most important components of a service, in a manner that supports the CSI Improvement Process. They can also centralize, automate and integrate the key processes. This then produces new data for trend analysis.

Tools to be used for CSI are for example:
- **IT service management suites** - tools and suites that are compatible with the ITIL process framework providing significant levels of integration between the processes and their associated record types. This functionality creates a rich source of data and creates many of the inputs for CSI. The Configuration Management System (CMS) is the foundation for the integration of all ITSM tool functionality and is a critical data source for CSI.
- **event management** - events are status messages from, for example, servers and systems; tools for event management assess these status reports for impact and origin, and categorize the reports
- **system and network management** - monitors technology platforms; the tools generate error messages for event management, providing input to performance management

- **automated incident and problem solving** - proactive detection monitors, pre-programmed scripts that automatically repair the technology; they also record information for analysis for possible improvements
- **knowledge management** - databases with descriptions of earlier incidents and problems, and their proven solutions; also measurement of the use of the database and the effectiveness of the solution
- **service request and fulfillment (service catalogue and workflow)** - helps with defining a service catalogue and automates service requests and their settlement
- **performance management** - collects data about availability, capacity and performance to develop availability and capacity information systems
- **application and service performance monitoring** - monitors the service of the technology from an end user perspective; the tools measure availability, reaction and transaction times and efficiency of the servers
- **statistical analysis tools** - central collection point for raw data from the above tools; the analysis instruments group these data logically, creating models for current services and making predictive models for future services
- **software version control/software configuration management** - creates an overview of all software for the development environment, thus providing the Definitive Media Library (DML)
- **software test management** - supports the test and roll-out activities of release management
- **security management** - protects against intruders and unauthorized use; all hardware and software that is under security management must automatically give a warning as soon as a security incident threatens
- **project and portfolio management** - registers new functionality and the services and systems that they support; the tools help to map the service portfolio and keep it up-to-date; they can also automate organizational aspects such as plans
- **financial management** - monitors the use of resources and services for the invoicing process
- **business intelligence/reporting** - collects data from all the above mentioned tools, with which it generates important information for the business

3.6 Implementation

Before you implement CSI you must make sure that:
- the critical roles of CSI manager, service owner and reporting analyst have been filled
- monitoring and reporting on technology metrics is in place

- internal review meetings are scheduled
- external review meeting scheduled to follow internal review meetings

Communication forms an important part of any service improvement project. A communications plan is required which will need to deal with the responses and feedback from the target audience.

Define a communication plan that always states the messenger, what is the message, target audience, timing and frequency of communication, method of communication and a feedback mechanism.

CSI can be implemented through various approaches:

- **service approach** - with this you define the issues with certain services; you create an action plan with the owner of the service: how are we going to remove the issue?
- **lifecycle approach** - with this you look at the results of the various lifecycle phases and you look for possible improvements
- **functional approach** - if many incidents occur with one specific function in an organization, for example in the server group, you can remove as many problems in this function group as possible with a test project

See also "Basic concepts": Organizational Change and the PDCA Cycle.

Business case

The business case must make it clear whether it is useful to start with CSI. It must indicate what exactly will change in the intended future situation with respect to the starting situation. From a set **baseline** an organization can estimate what the present situation provides and costs, and how much the improvement of the situation will provide and cost. Formulate this in the language that the business understands. In any case answer the following questions:

- **Where are we?** - Determine the present service levels.
- **What do we want?** - Determine the company vision, mission, goals and objectives.
- **What do we need?** - Determine what services are essential for the fulfillment of the mission and set priorities on the basis of this.
- **What can we afford?** - With the help of service level management (SLM) and financial management, set the budget for IT services and see what actions are feasible.
- **What will we get?** - Determine the required results together with the business
- **What did we get?** - Have Service Operation monitor the service levels and report on them.

- **Does it still meet our wants/needs?** - Look at further possible improvements with the business.

Answer these questions by testing. In the Section "Processes and other activities" testing is discussed in detail.

For a business case, it is important to have an overview of the **costs** and benefits of CSI. Extra information about the measurement and estimation of costs and benefits can be found in the Section "Processes and other activities" and in "Methods, techniques and tools".

Costs
When deciding on an improvement initiative, always keep an eye on the costs of development, operations and ongoing maintenance. Examples of this are:
- labor costs
- training costs
- tools to process measurement data
- assessments or benchmark studies
- management time to follow progress
- communication campaigns to create awareness and to change the culture

Benefits
Results of a service improvement plan can be divided into:
- **improvements** - measurable improvements with respect to the starting situation
- **benefits** - profit that is the result of improvements (usually in financial terms)
- **Return on Investment (ROI)** - the difference between the costs and benefits of the improvement
- **Value on Investment (VOI)** - ROI, plus the extra value that cannot be expressed in money or that only becomes clear in the long-term; it is difficult to quantify extra value such as higher customer satisfaction; if there are enough "hard numbers", it still does not add much; a narrative appendix as to this qualitative value is more useful

Define both direct and indirect benefits and consider each group of **stakeholders** for each organizational level. Define the benefits such that they are measurable. Put the business first. Added value for the business can mean:
- shorter time to market
- customer bonding

- lower maintenance costs for the inventory
- larger market share

CSI can provide the following benefits:
- **to the business**:
    - more reliable support for business processes through incident, problem and change management
    - higher productivity through increased quality and availability of IT services
    - the business knows what they can expect of the IT department and what the IT department expects of them
    - procedures to ensure the continuity of IT service are oriented to the needs of the business
    - better management information about business processes and IT services
    - the IT department has more knowledge of the business processes, so that it can respond better to the desires of the business
    - quality projects, releases and changes run according to plan and provide the agreed quality at the agreed costs
    - minimal number of unused opportunities
    - better relationship between the business and IT
    - higher customer satisfaction
- **financial**:
    - efficient IT services
    - cost effective IT infrastructure and services
    - cost reduction, for example though lower costs for the implementation of changes and less excess processes and equipment
    - changes have less (financial) impact on the business
    - services meet the requirements but do not over perform
    - better division of resources, such that expenditures for the continuity of IT services are in proportion with the importance of the business processes that they support
    - cost structure is tuned to business needs
    - minimal costs and risks with checks that legislation is followed
- **innovative**:
    - more proactive development of technology and services through better information on the areas in which changes can lead to profits
    - the IT department reacts better to changes in demands from the business or the market and to new trends
    - a business who trusts his IT service providers dares to "think big"

- **internal benefits for the IT organization**:
    - more competent IT department, less chance of errors
    - integration of people and processes
    - more communication and teamwork (also with the business)
    - more productive and more motivated staff
    - defined roles and responsibilities
    - more effective processes, better use of resources
    - IT repeats and increases profit points through increased process maturity
    - better metrics and management reports through structured approach to measurement and knowledge gathering
    - better picture of and more trust in present and future IT improvement opportunities
    - services and systems achieve feasible goals within a realistic schedule
    - better direction of service providers
    - better relationship with the business
    - cost alignment with business needs

Critical Success Factors (CSFs)

A **Critical Success Factor** (CSF) is a necessary condition for a good result of a service or process. Critical success factors for CSI are:
- appoint a **CSI manager** (see also "Organization")
- adoption of CSI by the whole organization
- constant visible management participation in CSI activities, for example by creating a vision and communicating about it
- clear criteria for the prioritization of improvement projects
- adoption of the service cycle approach
- sufficient funding
- resource allocation - people are dedicated to the improvement effort not just as an add-on to their already long list of tasks to perform
- technology to support improvement activities
- embrace service management processes and do not adapt it to meet personal needs and agendas

Challenges and risks

Introduction of CSI comes with the following challenges and risks:
- lack of management commitment
- poor relationship and communication between IT and the business
- too little knowledge of the IT impact on the business and its important processes
- too little knowledge of the business' priorities

- lack of information, monitoring and measurement
- not using the information from reports
- insufficient resources, budget and time
- immature service management processes
- too little or no knowledge management (see also "Organization")
- trying to change everything at once
- resistance against (cultural) changes
- not enough business or IT objectives, strategies and policy
- poor supplier management
- not testing
- tooling is too complex or too few
- difference in used technology

Interfaces

CSI uses a lot of data from the entire lifecycle of a service. The information that results from this, together with the demands of the business, the technical specifications, the opportunities of IT, the budget, trends and legislation, gives insight into the opportunities for the improvement of an organization.

Service Level Management (SLM)

Service level management is the most important process for CSI: it discusses with the business what the IT organization needs to measure and what the results should be. That is why this section begins with information on what SLM and CSI have in common.

After each phase of the lifecycle, test whether the improvement initiative has met its goals. This can be done using the **Post Implementation Review (PIR)** from the change management process.

Because steps 1 and 2 of the CSI improvement process lie primarily with SLM and CSI, an overview of the common ground between CSI and the other ITIL processes and the different Service Lifecycle phases is given starting from step 3 only. Service Operation also provides information about what *can* be measured before step 2.

In the light of CSI, the objective of SLM is to maintain and improve the quality of IT services. SLM does this by making a constant cycle of agreements, monitoring and reporting about IT service levels.

In the CSI improvement process, SLM plays a role with:

1. **What you should measure**:
   - consult with the business as to what it would like
2. **What you can measure**:
   - see what has already been measured
   - determine what can and should be measured (SLA, OLAs and Underpinning Contracts)
3. **Data gathering (measurement)**:
   - determine what happens with the data: who receives them, what analyses are needed?
4. **Data processing**:
   - evaluate the processed data from the business perspective
   - consider how often the data must be processed and how often they must be reported on
5. **Data analysis**:
   - compare the Service Level achievements (performance, results) with the SLAs
   - identify and record trends to expose possible patterns
   - determine the need for SIPs
   - the need to adjust existing OLAs or Underpinning Contracts (UCs)
6. **Presenting the information**:
   - reporting to and communicating with the business
   - organizing internal and external service evaluations
   - helping to prioritize activities
7. **Implementing corrective actions**:
   - together with problem and availability management, set up an SIP and ensure that the organization carries out this plan

In this way SLM determines what the organization measures and monitors together with the business, it reports on the performance and signals new business demands. Using this information CSI identifies and prioritizes improvement opportunities. This is the most important input for the SIP (Figure 3.7).

It is recommended that an annual budget is set for SIPs. SLM and CSI can then take quick action, which leads to a proactive attitude.

If an organization outsources its Service Delivery processes, it must also negotiate regarding CSI and include this in the SLA. Otherwise the acting party will no longer be motivated to deliver more than is agreed upon in the contract.

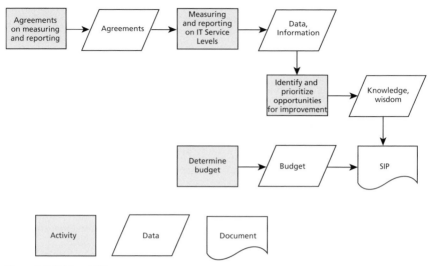

Figure 3.7 SLM and SIP

Monitor and gather data (measurement, step 4)
In the Service Lifecycle, *Service Strategy* monitors the effect of strategies, standards, policy and design decisions.

Service Design monitors and collects information related to the design and modification of services and service management processes. This phase also tests whether the CSFs and KPIs agreed upon with the business are measurable and effective. They also determine what should be measured and set schedules and milestones for this.

Service Transition monitors and measures data about the actual usage of services and service management processes. It develops the monitoring procedures and sets measurement criteria for after implementation.

Service Operation measures the performance of the services and components in the production environment. Once again this forms input for the CSI improvement process: what can be measured and what do these data say?

Apart from SLM, availability management also plays an important role in step 3. This process:
- creates metrics in consultation with the business to measure availability
- determines which tools are needed to make these measurements

- monitors and measures the performance of the infrastructure and frees up enough resources for this
- provides data to CSI
- updates availability plans

Capacity management also undertakes these actions; it does this in order to measure whether the IT organization can provide the requested services. This can be done from three perspectives:
- **business capacity management** - answers the question "what do we need?" and "how to we measure that?" together with the business
- **service capacity management** - answers the question "what do we need?" from the service perspective and provides information about this to CSI
- **component capacity management** - looks at the components a service is built up of and what needs to be measured to monitor this in its entirety

Incident management defines monitoring requirements to track events and incidents, preferably automated, before they cause problems. It also monitors the reaction, repair, and resolution time and the number of escalations. For example, the service desk monitors the number of reports, the average response time and the percentage of callers who hang up prematurely.

Security management monitors and measures the security and records security incidents and problems.

And, finally, financial management monitors and measures the costs and keeps an eye on the budget. It also contributes to the reports as to the costs and ROI of improvement initiatives.

Process data (step 4)
Service Operation processes the data in logical groups. Within these groups availability management and capacity management process the data at the component level regarding availability and capacity. They work together with SLM to give these data an "end-to-end" perspective and use the agreed upon reporting form to do this.

Incident management and service desk check and process data about incidents and service requests, and the KPIs related to this. Security management checks and processes data about security incidents and reports on them.

Analyze data (step 5)
Service Strategy analyzes trends, looks at whether the strategies, policy and standards introduced achieve their goal, and whether there are opportunities for improvement. *Service Design* analyzes the results of design and project activities, and researches trends and opportunities for improvement. It also looks at whether the CSFs and KPIs set in step 2 are still adequate. *Service Operation* also analyzes results, trends and opportunities for improvement.

The most important Service Operation process for CSI is problem management. This process finds the underlying causes of problems, and these form important opportunities for improvement.

Availability management analyzes performance and trends about components and service data. It compares data with earlier months, quarters and years. It also looks at whether the correct information is being measured and whether SIPs are needed. It uses the following techniques:

- **Component Failure Impact Analysis (CFIA)** - an availability matrix updates which components are strategically important for each service and what role they play (Figure 3.8); a well-arranged configuration management database (CMDB) is required for this; identifies single points of failure
- **Fault Tree Analysis (FTA)** - determines the chain of events that can lead to the failure of an IT service (Figure 3.9)
- **Service Failure Analysis (SFA)** - looks at what a failure means for the business (impact) and what the business expects and aims at end-to-end availability improvement; on the basis of this, CSI can determine and prioritize possible improvements
- **Technical Observation Post (TOP)** - a meeting of IT personnel with different specializations to discuss one aspect of availability
- **Expanded Incident Lifecycle** - calculates the mean time to restore a service (MTRS)

Capacity management analyzes when which customer uses what services, how they use them and how this influences the performance of one or more systems or components. This again provides improvement opportunities to CSI.

Whereas problem management is oriented toward resolving problems that have already occurred in the past, capacity management tries to prevent problems proactively, by making extra storage capacity ready on time, for example. Often this is done by reproducing the situation in a model, and then asking a number of "what if" questions.

Configuration Item:	Service A	Service B
PC #1	B	B
PC #2		B
Cable #1	B	B
Cable #2		B
Outlet #1	X	X
Outlet #2		X
Ethernet segment	X	X
Router	X	X
Wan Link	X	X
Router	X	X
Segment	X	X
NIC	A	A
Server	B	B
System software	B	B
Application	B	B
Database	X	X

X = Fault means service is unavailable
A = Failsafe configuration
B = Failsafe, with changeover time
" " = No impact

Figure 3.8 CFIA matrix

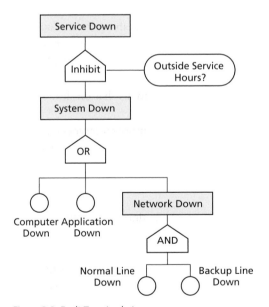

Figure 3.9 Fault Tree Analysis

Incident management and the service desk can compare the collected data with earlier results and the agreed service levels. They can also propose SIPs or corrective actions.

Security management uses all the other processes to find the origin of security incidents and problems. It looks for trends and possible improvements in the area of monitoring and looks at whether security strategies produce the intended results.

Every improvement initiative must consult IT Service Continuity Management (ITSCM) to make sure that the IT services are not put at risk. **Risk management** plays a central role in this. It analyzes what effects an improvement can have, while in turn CSI analyzes the results of risk management activities, to discover opportunities for improvement. See also Service Design regarding risk management.

Present and use (step 6)

Service Strategy presents results, trends and recommendations for the improvement of adopted strategies, policy and standards. *Service Design* does this for design improvements and project activities and *Service Transition* and *Service Operation* for service and service management processes.

Availability management, capacity management, incident management, service desk, problem management, and security management help with creating reports and prioritizing corrective actions.

Knowledge management is very important in presenting and using the information for CSI. This is the only way CSI can get a good overview of the knowledge of the organization and the opportunities for improvement. It is also important in order to ensure continual improvement and that all the knowledge and experience gathered is shared and stored.

Implement corrective actions (step 7)

Availability management, capacity management, incident management, service desk, problem management and security management perform incremental or corrective actions where approval from the business is not required.

Capacity management can also proceed by introducing **demand management** measures to influence the behavior of the end user:
* calculation of costs
* making policy for the proper use of the services
* communicating expectations
* education about proper use
* negotiating maintenance times
* setting use restrictions, such as limiting the amount of storage space

As with all other changes in the lifecycle, CSI changes must go through the change, release, and deployment process. CSI must therefore submit a Request for Change (RFC) with change management and conduct a PIR after implementation. Also consider the updating of the CMDB by means of configuration management. After this, IT Service Continuity Management (ITSCM) must keep the continuity plan up-to-date.

Finally

The introduction of CSI is not simple. It requires conscious striving toward continual improvement as part of the culture and behavior of the organization, and a proactive attitude. In a world where the technology changes very quickly, such a proactive attitude is a big challenge; after all we are constantly controlled by the changes. In a situation of increasing outsourcing and professional development of IT service management, service quality is progressively becoming a distinguishing factor. To get "in control" and to achieve the desired quality it is preferable to work proactively. CSI is essential to this.

As with many other domains, a step-by-step approach is needed for this. Do not begin with a big-bang approach with all the processes at once, but first determine the biggest problem areas (for example with SWOT) and choose a well-considered approach for the improvements. Recognizing the critical success factors is very important here.

CHAPTER 4

Introduction to Functions and Processes

4.1 Introduction

Processes are *internal* affairs for the IT service provider. An organization that is still trying to gain control of its processes therefore has an **internal focus**. Organizations that focus on gaining control of their systems in order to provide services are still internally focused. The organization is not ready for an **external focus** until it controls its services and is able to vary them on request. This external focus is required to evolve into that desirable customer-focused organization.

Because organizations can be in different stages of maturity, IT managers require a broad orientation in their discipline. Most organizations are now working on the introduction of a process-focused or customer-focused approach, or still have to start working on this. Process control is therefore a vital step on the road towards a **mature customer-focused organization**.

ITIL has made an important contribution to the organization of that process-focused operating method in the past decade. The development started in North-western Europe and has made some progress on most other continents in the last few years also. On a global scale, however, a minimal number of organizations have actually started with this approach - and an even smaller number have made serious progress at this point. The organization change projects that were thought to be necessary to convert to a process-focused organization were not all successful.

These findings lead us to conclude that the majority of organizations in the world require access to good information and best practices concerning the **business processes of**

IT organizations. Fortunately, that information is abundant. The ITIL version 2 books provide comprehensive documentation on the most important processes, while ITIL version 3 adds even more information.

The **process model** is at least as important as the processes because processes must be deployed in the right relationships to achieve the desired effect of a process-focused approach. There are many different process models available. The experiences gained with these processes and process models in recent years have been documented comprehensively in books, magazines and white papers, and have been presented at countless conventions.

4.2 Management of processes

Every organization aims to realize its vision, mission, strategy, objectives and policies, which means that appropriate activities have to be undertaken.

For example, a restaurant will have to purchase fresh ingredients, the chefs will have to work together to provide consistent results, and there should be no major differences in style among the waiting staff. A restaurant will only be awarded a three-star rating when it manages to provide the same high quality over an extended period of time. This is not always the case: there will be changes among the waiting staff, a successful approach may not last, and chefs often leave to open their own restaurants. Providing consistently high quality means that the component activities have to be coordinated: the better and more efficiently the kitchen operates, the higher the quality of service that can be provided to the guests.

In the example of the restaurant, appropriate activities include buying vegetables, bookkeeping, ordering publicity material, receiving guests, cleaning tables, peeling potatoes and making coffee. With just such an unstructured list, something will be left out and staff will easily become confused. It is therefore a better idea to structure the activities. Preferably these will be structured in such a way as to allow us to see how each group of activities contributes to the objectives of the business, and how they are related to other activities.

Such groups of activities are known as **processes**. If the process structure of an organization is clearly described, it will show:
- what has to be done
- what the expected inputs and results are
- how we measure whether the processes deliver the expected results
- how the results of one process affect those of another process

Processes can be defined in many ways. Depending upon the objectives of the creator, more or less emphasis will be on specific aspects. For example, a highly detailed process description will allow for a high level of control. Superficial process definitions will illustrate that the creator does not care much about the way in which the steps are executed.

Once the processes are defined, the roles, responsibilities and people can be assigned to specific aspects, bringing the process to the level of a *procedure*.

Processes

When arranging activities into processes, we do not use the existing allocation of tasks, nor the existing departmental divisions. This is a conscious choice. By opting for a process structure, it often becomes evident that certain activities in the organization are uncoordinated, duplicated, neglected or unnecessary.

> A **process** is a structured set of activities designed to accomplish a defined objective.

Instead, we look at the **objective** of the process and the **relationships** with other processes. A process is a series of activities carried out to convert input into an output, and ultimately into an outcome. The **input** is concerned with the resources being used in the process. The (reported) **output** describes the immediate results of the process, while the **outcome** indicates the long-term results of the process (in terms of meaningful effect). Through **control** activities, we can associate the input and output of each of the processes with **policies and standards** to provide information about the results to be obtained by the process. Control regulates the input and the **throughput** in case the throughput or output parameters are not compliant with these standards and policies. This produces chains of processes that show the input that goes into the organization and what the result, and it also monitors points in the chains in order to check the quality of the products and services provided by the organization.

The standards for the output of each process have to be defined, in such a way that the complete chain of processes in the process model meets the corporate objective. If the output of a process meets the defined requirements, then the process is **effective** in transforming its input into its output. To be really effective, the outcome should be taken into consideration rather than merely focusing on the output. If the activities in the process are also carried out with the minimum required effort and cost, then the process is **efficient**. It is the task of process management to use **planning and control** to ensure that processes are executed in an effective and efficient way.

We can study each process separately to optimize its quality. The **process owner** is responsible for the process results. The **process manager** is responsible for the realization and structure of the process, and reports to the process owner.

The logical combination of activities results in clear transfer points where the quality of processes can be monitored. In the restaurant example, we can separate responsibility for purchasing and cooking, so that the chefs do not have to purchase anything and can concentrate on their core activities.

The management of the organization can provide control on the basis of the process quality of the process as demonstrated by data from the results of each process. In most cases, the relevant **performance indicators** and standards will already be agreed upon. In this case the process manager can do the day-to-day control of the process. The process owner will assess the results based on a **report** of performance indicators and checks whether the results meet the agreed standard. Without clear indicators, it would be difficult for a process owner to determine whether the process is under control, and if planned improvements are being implemented.

Processes are often described using **procedures** and **work instructions**.

A **procedure** *is a specified way to carry out an activity or a process.*
A procedure describes the "how", and can also describe "who" carries the activities out. A procedure may include stages from different processes. A procedure can vary depending on the organization.

*A set of **work instructions** defines how one or more activities in a procedure should be carried out in detail, using technology or other resources.*

A process is defined as a logically related series of activities executed to meet the goals of a defined objective. Processes are composed of two kinds of activities: the activities to realize the goal (operational activities concerned with the throughput), and the activities to manage these (control activities). The control activities make sure the operational activities (the workflow) are performed in time, in the right order, etc. (For example, in the processing of changes it is always ensured that a test is performed *before* a release is taken into production and not *afterwards*.)

Processes and departments

Most businesses are hierarchically organized. There are departments that are responsible for the activities of a group of employees. There are various ways of structuring departments, such as by customer, product, region or discipline. IT services generally depend on several departments, customers or disciplines. For example, if there is an IT service to provide users with access to an accounting program on a central computer, this will involve several disciplines. The computer center has to make the program and database accessible, the data and telecommunications department has to make the computer center accessible, and the PC support team has to provide users with an interface to access the application.

Processes that span several departments (teams) can monitor the quality of a service by monitoring particular aspects of quality, such as availability, capacity, cost and stability. A service organization will try to match these quality aspects with the customer's demands. The structure of such processes can ensure that good information is available about the provision of services, so that the planning and control of services can be improved.

Figure 4.1 shows a basic example of the combinations of activities in a process (indicated by the dashed lines).

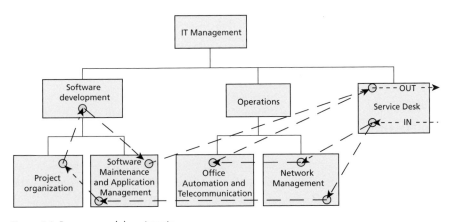

Figure 4.1 Processes and departments

IT service management and processes

IT service management has been known as the process and service-focused approach of what was initially known as Information Technology management. The shift of management from infrastructure to processes has paved the way for the term IT service management as a process and customer-focused discipline. Processes should always have a defined objective. The objective of IT service management processes is to contribute to the quality of the IT services. Quality management and process control are part of the organization and its policies.

By using a process approach, best practices for IT service management describe how services can be delivered, using the most effective and efficient series of activities. The Service Lifecycle in ITIL V3 is based on these process descriptions. The structure and allocation of tasks and responsibilities between functions and departments depends on the type of organization, and these structures vary widely among IT departments, and they often change. The description of the process structure however, provides a common point of reference that changes less rapidly. This can help to maintain the quality of IT services during and after reorganizations, and also among service providers and partners as they change. This makes service providers far less sensitive to organizational change, and much more flexible: providers can continually adapt their organization to changing conditions, leaving the core of their processes in place. In this way the shop can stay open during reconstruction work. However, reality may pose some practical problems, making this more difficult in practice than it seems in theory.

Applying the best process definitions of the industry allows IT service providers to concentrate on their business. As with other fields of industry, the processes in the IT industry are similar for all organizations of the same nature. Many of the process descriptions documented in ITIL have been recognized as the best that the industry could hope to adopt.

4.3   Teams, roles and positions in ITSM

Organizations divide the various tasks for carrying out processes or activities in many different ways. Tasks can be covered by organizational bodies, such as groups, teams, departments or divisions. These organizational bodies are then managed in **hierarchical organizations** by a line manager, who has a certain "span of control" and who manages one or more of these bodies. **Flat organizations** have relatively few layers in this hierarchy. Organizations can also divide the tasks more in the spirit of equality, such as, for example, **network organizations**, in which the cooperation between the various bodies is paramount.

Besides hierarchical organizations, which manage through "the line", there are also **project organizations**, which manage primarily by using temporary forms of project cooperation, while **process organizations** are managed primarily by means of an agreed work method. Obviously, these types of management can be combined in innumerable ways. As a result of this, we are seeing a great number of unique organizational configurations in the field.

Organizations can distinguish themselves from other organizations, particularly in respect to the type of organization they operate. An organization that is directed toward hierarchy will have a staff primarily of senior line management. A process-oriented organization will have staff that are responsible for processes. Depending on the degree to which management is based on processes, the line or projects, the staff will consist of a mix of the relevant responsible managers.

When setting up an organization, positions and roles are also used, in addition to the various groups (teams, departments, divisions). **Roles** are sets of responsibilities, activities and authorities granted to a person or team. One person or team may have multiple roles; for example, the roles of Configuration Manager and Change Manager may be carried out by a single person. **Positions** (functions) are traditionally recognized as tasks and responsibilities that are assigned to a specific person. A person in a particular position has a clearly defined package of tasks and responsibilities which may include various roles. Positions can also be more broadly defined as a logical concept that refers to the people and automated measures that carry out a clearly defined process, an activity or a combination of processes or activities.

4.4 Tools used in ITSM

In the performance of tasks in IT service management, innumerable automated support aids can be used: these are referred to as tools. With the help of these tools, management tasks can be automated; for example, monitoring tasks or software distribution tasks. Other tools support the performance of the activities themselves; for example, service desk tools or service management tools. The latter category, in fact, supports the management of several processes and are therefore often referred to as workflow tools - although they may not have actual workflow engines.

The fact that the IT field is fundamentally focused on automated facilities (for information processing) has led to a virtual deluge of tools appearing on the market, which have greatly increased the performance capacity of IT organizations.

4.5   Communication in IT service organizations

People, process, partners and technology provide the main "machinery" of any organization, but they only work well if the machine is oiled: **communication** is an essential element in any organization. If the people do not know about the processes or use the wrong instructions or tools, the output may not be as anticipated.

People are core assets of the organization. This is not only due to the fact that they need to be in place to perform certain activities or to take decisions, but also because people have the good habit of communicating. When an organization applies highly detailed instructions for all its activities, it will end up in a bureaucracy. On the other hand, an organization without any rules is will most likely end up in chaos. Whichever balance an organization is trying to find here, it will always benefit enormously from communication between the people in the organization. A regular and formal meeting culture will support this, but organizations should not underestimate the important role of informal communication: many projects have been saved by means of a simple chat in the tea room, or in the car park.

Formal structures on communication include:
- **reporting** - internal and external reporting, aimed at management or customers, project progress reports, alerts
- **meetings** - formal project meetings, regular meetings with specific targets
- **online facilities** - email systems, chat-rooms, pagers, groupware, document sharing systems, messenger facilities, teleconferencing and virtual meeting facilities
- **notice boards** - near the coffee maker, water cooler, at the entrance of the building, in the company restaurant

IT teams and departments, as well as users, internal customers and service production teams, must communicate with each other. The **stakeholders** for communication can thus be found among all managers and employees who are involved in service management, in all the layers of the organization, and with all customers, users and service providers. Good communication can prevent problems. All communication must have a particular goal or result. Every team, process and every department must have a clear **communications policy**.

IT service management includes several types of communication, such as:
- routine operational communication
- communication between teams
- performance reports
- communication during projects

- communication when there are changes
- communication in case of exceptions
- communication in case of emergencies
- training for new or adapted processes and service designs
- communication with service production teams regarding service strategies and design

4.6 Culture

Organizations that want to change, for example to improve the quality of their services, will eventually be confronted with the current organizational culture and will have to deal with any changes to this culture as a consequence of the overall change. The organizational culture, or corporate culture, refers to the way in which people deal with each other in the organization; the way in which decisions are made and implemented; and the attitude of employees to their work, customers, service providers, superiors and colleagues.

Culture, which depends on the standards and values of the people in the organization, cannot be controlled, but it can be influenced. Influencing the culture of an organization requires leadership in the form of a clear and consistent policy, as well as a supportive personnel policy.

The corporate culture can have a major influence on the provision of IT services. Businesses value innovation in different ways. In a stable organization, where the culture places little value on innovation, it will be difficult to adjust its IT services in line with changes in the organization of the customer. If the IT department is unstable, then a culture which values change can pose a serious threat to the quality of its services. In that case, a "free for all" culture can develop where many uncontrolled changes lead to a large number of faults.

4.7 Processes, projects, programs and portfolios

Activities can be managed from a process perspective, from an organizational hierarchy (line) perspective, from a project perspective, or from any combination of these three. Organizations that tend to apply just one of these management systems often miss the benefits of the others. The practical choice often depends upon history, culture, available skills and competences, and personal preferences. The optimum choice may be entirely different, but the requirements for applying this optimum may be hard to realize and vary in time.

There are no "hard and fast laws" for the way an organization should combine processes, projects and programs. However, it is generally accepted that there are some consequences attached to modern practices in IT service organizations, since the most widely accepted approach to service management is based on process management. This means that whenever the organization works with projects or programs, it should have established how these approaches work together.

The practical relationship between projects and processes is determined by the relative position of both in terms of "leading principles for the management of the organization": if projects are considered more important than processes, then decisions on projects will overrule decisions on processes; as a consequence, the organization will not be able to implement a stable set of processes. If it is the other way around, with projects only able to run within the constraints of agreed processes, then project management will be a discipline that will have to adapt to new boundaries and definitions (e.g. since projects always change something from A to B, they will most likely fall under the regime of Change, Release and Deployment Management).

The most suitable solution is dependent upon the understanding of the role of IT service management in the organization. To be able to find a solution for this management challenge, it is recommended that a common understanding of processes, projects, programs, and even portfolio's is created. The following definitions may be used:
- **Process** - A process is a structured set of activities designed to accomplish a defined objective.
- **Project** - A project is a temporary organization, with people and other assets required to achieve an objective.
- **Program** - A program consists of a number of projects and activities that are planned and managed together to achieve an overall set of related objectives.
- **Portfolio** - A portfolio is a set of projects and/or programs, which are not necessarily related, brought together for the sake of control, coordination and optimization of the portfolio in its totality. NB: In ITIL, a service portfolio is the complete set of services that are managed by a service provider.

Since the project/program/portfolio grouping is a hierarchical set of essential project resources, the issue can be downscaled to that of a relationship between a project and a process.
The most elementary difference between a process and a project is the one-off character of a project, versus the continuous character of the process. If a project has achieved its objectives, it means the end of the project. Processes can be run many times, both in parallel and in sequence. The nature of a process is aimed at its repeatable character:

processes are defined only in case of a repeatable string of activities that are important enough to be standardized and optimized.

Projects are aimed at changing a situation A into a situation B. This can involve a simple string of activities, but it can also be a very complex series of activities. Other elements of importance for projects include money, time, quality, organization and information. Project structures are normally used only if at least one of these elements is of considerable value.

Actually, projects are just ways of organizing a specific change in a situation. In that respect they have a resemblance with processes. It is often a matter of focus: processes focus at the specific sequence of activities, the decisions taken at certain milestone stages, and the quality of the activities involved. Processes are continuously instantiated and repeated, and use the same approach each time. Projects focus more at the time and money constraints, in terms of resources spent on the change and the projects end, and projects vary much more than processes.

A very practical way of combining the benefits of both management systems might be as follows:
- Processes set the scene for how specific series of activities are performed.
- Projects can be used to transform situation A into situation B, and always refer to a change.
- If the resources (time, money, or other) involved in a specific process require the level of attention that is normally applied in a project, then (part of) the process activities can be performed as a project, but always under the control of the process: if changes are performed, using project management techniques, the agreed change management policies still apply.

This would allow organizations to maintain a continuous customer focus and apply a process approach to optimize this customer focus, and at the same time benefit from the high level of resource control that can be achieved when using project management techniques.

4.8 Functions and processes in the lifecycle phases

For the sake of readability and uniformity, the following structure for the descriptions was used as much as possible:
- **introduction** - describes the purpose and aims of the process or function, its scope, value to the business, principles, guidelines, starting points and basic concepts

- **activities, methods and techniques** - explains the process or function in greater detail based on the workflow of activities (if possible); also describes commonly used methods and techniques
- **interfaces** - describes how the process or function is triggered, its inputs and outputs, and its links to other functions and processes
- **metrics** - describes the process metrics, in particular the Key Performance Indicators (KPIs)
- **implementation** - describes the Critical Success Factors (CSFs), challenges, risks and traps that may apply for the introduction of a process or function

CHAPTER 5

Functions and Processes in Continual Service Improvement

5.1 CSI Improvement Process

Introduction

The **CSI improvement process** or **7-step improvement process** describes how to measure and report. Improvement takes place according to the PDCA Cycle. The CSI plan phase results in a **Service Improvement Plan (SIP)**. The next section will explain how an organization can set up such a plan.

Activities, methods and techniques

If service level management discovers that something could improve, they will pass this on to CSI. CSI can think up activities to accomplish these improvements. CSI will create an SIP for execution purposes. This will turn "improvement" into an IT process with input, activities, output, roles and reports.

CSI will measure and process these measurements in a continual improvement process (Figure 5.1). This will take place in **seven steps from measurement to improvement**:

1. **What *should* you measure?** - What would be the ideal situation? This must follow from the vision (Phase I of the CSI model) and precede the assessment of the current situation (Phase II of the CSI model).
2. **What *can* you measure?** - This step follows from Phase III of the CSI model: where do we want to be? By researching what the organization can measure, it will discover new business requirements and new IT options. By using a *gap analysis* CSI can find areas for improvement and plan these (Phase IV of the CSI model).

3. **Gather data (measure)** - In order to verify whether the organization has reached its goal (Phase V of the CSI model), it must perform measurements. The measurements must follow from its vision, mission, goals and objectives.
4. **Process data** - The processing of data is also necessary for monitoring purposes. This must happen according to CSFs and KPIs determined.
5. **Analyze data** - Discrepancies, trends and possible explanations are prepared for presentation to the business. This is also an important part of Phase V of the CSI model.
6. **Present and use information** - This is where the stakeholder is informed whether his goals have been achieved (still Phase V).
7. **Implement corrective action** - Create improvements, establish a new baseline and start the cycle from the top.

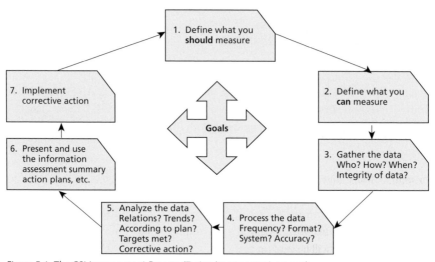

Figure 5.1 The CSI Improvement Process (7-step improvement process)

The cycle is preceded and closed by **identification of vision and goals** *(identify)*. This is where the vision, strategy, tactical and operational goals are charted. This step returns in Phase I of the CSI model: determine the vision. Figure 5.2 shows how the CSI model and the CSI improvement process mesh together.

Steps 1 and 2 should be the direct result of the strategic, tactical and operational goals of the organization. They are iterative: in every step you should question whether you are measuring what you should be measuring and whether the measured values are reliable

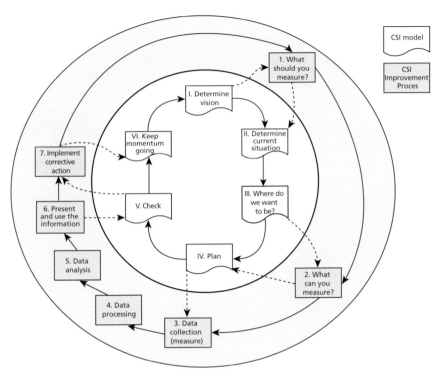

Figure 5.2 Connection between CSI Model and CSI Improvement Process

and useful. Answer these questions together with the business in order to be sure that you will be able to provide it with useful information in Step 6.

If no **baseline** has yet been determined, that measurement must take place first. The first measuring results will be the baseline. Every level should be charted in this process: strategic goals and objectives, tactical process maturity and operational **metrics** and KPIs. In this way, a knowledge spiral develops: the information from Step 6 in the operational level is input for Step 3 (gather data) of the tactical level, and information from the tactical level will provide data to the strategic level (Figure 5.3).

If there is little data available, you must first determine a basic measurement system. Start collecting consistent data, for example by having IT staff record data in the same way. You can also measure the process maturity of current processes to discover those processes that deviate most from *best practice*. However, this will only show a lack of data, you will not be collecting any new information in this way.

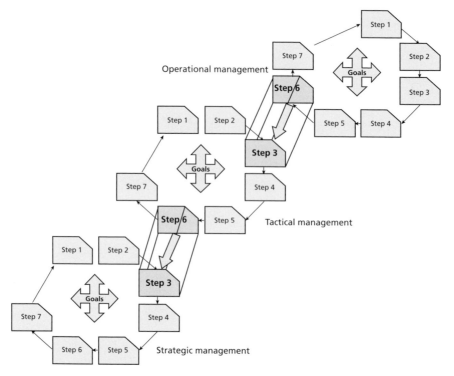

Figure 5.3 Knowledge spiral

Never allow "measuring" to become a goal unto itself. Before a manager decides what he will be measuring and for how long, he should contemplate why he should measure and how he will put the results to use. This depends on the goal of the manager. The four most common reasons to measure are:

- **validate** - to test prior decisions
- **direct** - set direction to activities in order to reach goals
- **justify** - support for the necessity of a certain action
- **intervene** - determine a point at which corrective actions or changes in the process are required

It is always important to keep sight of these reasons, including while measuring is taking place. After every report, the manager should wonder: "do we (still) need this?" The questions "what am I really measuring?" and "how will I retrieve that information?" are also very important, they should return at every step.

The responsibility for this lies with the owner of every dashboard, they must create useful reports and make sure that the (customer) organization actually uses them.

If you follow the seven steps of the improvement process, these questions will appear by themselves. More details about these steps follow below.

Step 1 - What should you measure?

In a perfect world, the **service owners** determine what they should measure. For this reason, they will chart the activities that are needed for the service management processes, or to provide services. Then they plan which measurements will show whether the services actually provide what was agreed with the business, and the way in which they can measure whether processes are proceeding smoothly.

The final list should reflect the visions, missions, goals and objectives of the business and IT, synchronized to each other. This should result in a number of CSFs, as well as *Service Level Targets*. The job descriptions of IT staff should also be related to this.

Have discussions with the business and the service providers for this purpose, and use the service catalogue and *Service Level Requirements* (SLRs) as starting points. Determine priorities based on the business priorities. In this, also remember internal and external service providers: what of theirs should you be measuring in order to determine whether you can provide your service?

Input for Step 1:
- service level requirements and goals
- service catalogue
- vision, mission, goals and objectives of the organization as a whole, and of the various units
- legal requirements
- governance requirements
- budget
- balanced scorecard

The **output** of Step 1 is a list of what you should be measuring, including:
- CSFs
- KPIs
- metrics
- measurements

Step 2 - What can you measure?

There may be a discrepancy between your "ideal list" from Step 1 and actual options. Based on existing tools, organizational culture and process maturity, determine what you can measure.

Chart what has been measured, which reports and databases the organization is generating and whether these are kept up-to-date. Also determine the risk if you decide not to measure something: how does that compare to the costs of the measurement? If you are unable to measure something, it should not be included in the SLA.

Finally, determine the differences between the "ideal list" and the list with possible measurements. It is possible that existing tools must be adjusted, or that new tools are required in order to move closer to the ideal list.

More information about CSFs and KPIs can be found under "Basic concepts" in the Section about CSI in Chapter 3 ("Metrics and KPIs"). Step 4 in the CSI process, process data, also provides additional information.

Input for Step 2:
- list including what to measure from Step 1, including CSFs, KPIs and metrics
- process flows
- procedures
- work instructions
- technical and user manuals for existing tools
- existing reports

Output of Step 2:
- list of what can be measured, including CSFs, KPIs and metrics
- list of required adjustments to tools
- list of required new tools

Step 3 - Gather data (measuring)

Steps 1 and 2 will indicate which data is required and measurable. Define measurements according to SMART. In order to collect data, you must **monitor**. This can be done using tools, but also manually. Monitoring should be focused on a service, process, tool, organization or CI. This does not always have to relate to infrastructure. It might also focus on discovering the degree to which staff are complying to a process.

CSI stresses discovery of areas for improvement. These are often exceptions to the rule, such as unsolved incidents. Both tools, as well as people, can provide warnings regarding exceptions.

If an organization consistently meets an SLAs requirement, CSI can also see if they can reach the same level for lower costs or whether they might be able to provide a higher level of service.

The design of a new service or adjustment to an existing service is the perfect occasion to include the monitoring requirements in the service requirements.

Business requirements for monitoring will change over time. This is why Service Operation and CSI must design a process that will help business and IT reach an agreement about what should be monitored and why.

If staff are collecting data **manually**, they must agree to the following:
- Who is responsible for monitoring and collecting data?
- How will data be collected?
- When and how often will data be collected?
- Which criteria guarantee the correctness and reliability of data?

Data gathering consists of the following **activities**:
- based on the SIP, goals, objectives and business requirements, specify which process activities you must monitor:
  specify monitoring requirements
  define requirements for data collection
  record results
  apply for approval from the internal IT department
- determine how and how often you want to collect data
- determine which tools are required, develop or buy these, or customize existing tools
- test and install the tool
- write monitoring procedures and work instructions
- create a monitoring plan and discuss it; ask for approval from internal and external IT service providers
- realize availability and capacity planning
- start monitoring and gathering data
- organize the data in a logical fashion in a report
- evaluate data in order to be sure that it is correct and useful

Input for Step 3:
- list stating what you should measure
- list stating what you can measure
- list stating what you will be measuring
- existing SLAs
- new business requirements
- existing monitoring and data gathering options
- availability and capacity planning
- SIPs
- prior trend analyses
- gap analysis report
- customer satisfaction studies

Output for Step 3:
- current availability and capacity planning
- monitoring plan
- monitoring procedures
- selected tools
- data concerning the ability by IT to meet business expectations
- data collection
- agreement on the reliability and applicability of data

If it turns out that data collected cannot be used or is unreliable, at least put it to use analyzing which data will be needed. For this purpose, repeat steps one and two.

Step 4 - Process data

Here you will process the raw data from Step 3 into the required format for the target audience. Follow the path from metric via KPI to CSF, right back to the vision if necessary (Figure 5.4).

Translate the data into a depiction of the service performance from a business perspective. The business is not interested in knowing that a server was available 99.99% of the time if it had no access to it. Collect data logically so that data analysis (Step 5) becomes easier. Tools can generate reports for this. At this point, data becomes *information*, according to the DIKW model.

Data processing consists of the following **activities**:
- define the requirements of the processed data based on strategy, goals and SLAs

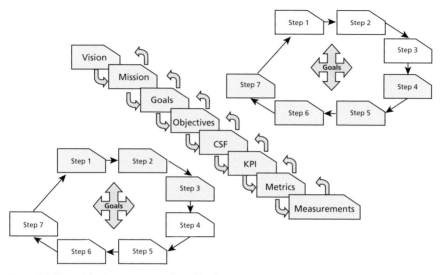

Figure 5.4 From vision to measurements and back

- determine how data is being processed; for new services or processes, it is preferable to select shorter intervals; is this by hour, day, week or month?
- determine the data grouping based on the method of analysis and target group; formulate requirements to tools, develop or buy them, test and install them
- develop procedures to process data, and train people in the procedures
- create a monitoring plan and discuss it; ask for approval from internal and external IT service providers
- update availability and capacity planning
- start data processing
- group the data in a logical fashion
- evaluate data accuracy

Input for Step 4:
- data gathered by monitoring
- reporting requirements
- SLAs and OLAs (Operational Level Agreements)
- service catalogue
- list with metrics, KPIs, CSF, objectives and goals
- reporting frequency
- reporting templates

Output for Step 4:
- current availability and capacity planning
- reports
- processed, logically grouped data ready for analysis

Step 5 - Analyze data
Without analysis, data is "only" information. It does not provide understanding of areas for improvement. Analysis evaluates whether IT services support the goals and objectives determined. The data will be applied to answer questions such as:
- Can clear trends be observed?
  - Are they positive or negative?
  - Are they in line with the goals?
  - Did we expect these trends?
  - What are potential explanations?
- Are changes necessary?
- Will we meet planning and goals?
- Are there structural, underlying problems?

Discuss the answers to these questions internally with the IT department first, in order to discover improvement options in collaboration. For example, think of training, testing and documentation. A logical start is to discover the "weakest link": the least efficient process activity. This is often the place where the most profit can be gained.

Because of prior discussions about improvement options, IT will make the first move in the dialogue with the business that follows analysis. A good analysis of the information is also to the business' advantage. This will allow a more accurate determination of whether improvement is required on the basis of strategic, tactical and operational goals. At this point, information becomes *knowledge*, according to the DIKW model.

Step 6 - Present and use information (service reporting)
Step six, **service reporting** (see also Section 5.2 "Service reporting" for a more detailed description) must translate knowledge into *wisdom* which is required to make strategic, tactical and operational decisions. Convincingly support with facts any added value IT will have for the business. For this purpose, present information to various stakeholders, at all levels of the organization. Include the use of marketing and communication techniques. Adjust the message and method to **your target group and its requirements**. Normally, there are three possible target groups: the business, senior (IT) management, and the internal IT organization.

Staff members in different organizational levels have different requirements. Therefore, distinguish these by **staff members and their requirements**, such as strategic thinkers, directors, managers and supervisors, team leaders and staff.

In order to provide useful reports to a customer, these reports should be set up from a **business perspective**, which is to say, from an **end-to-end perspective** - a customer is not interested in details about the functioning of the technical infrastructure through which services are provided, but only in the service itself.

Take the time to set up a **reporting framework** together with the business and Service Design: a policy that is formulated according to the rules by which you report. Determine this per business unit, so that you can distinguish between, for example, production and sales departments. Once this has been determined, data can easily be translated into meaningful reports, sometimes even fully automated.

Step 7 - Implement corrective action
An organization will not be able to implement all of the determined improvement options immediately. For this reason, options should be assigned a **priority** based on the organizational goals and external regulations determined in the Service Strategy. After this, the Service Design can develop the improvements, after which Service Transition will roll them out in the live environment and Service Operation will incorporate daily operation. During the entire cycle, continue to measure, analyze and report in order to see whether SLAs and KPIs still meet requirements. In addition, continue to pay attention to communication, training and documentation.

In retrospect, measure whether desired improvements have produced the effect you expected in terms of profits, ROI and VOI. As a result, study whether additional improvement is necessary, and start over with Step 1.

5.2   Service Reporting

Introduction

The **service reporting process** is the process which is responsible for the generation and supply of reports about the results achieved and the developments in service levels. It should agree with the business on the lay-out, contents and frequency of the reports.

Figure 5.5 shows how the service reporting process converts knowledge into the *wisdom* which is needed to make strategic, tactical and operational decisions.

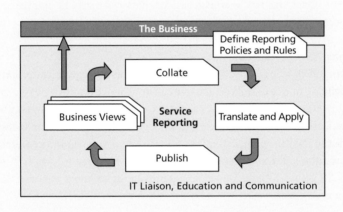

Figure 5.5 Service reporting process

Activities, methods and techniques

The service reporting process distinguishes the following activities:

* gather data
* process the data into information and apply this to the organization publish the information
* fine-tune the reporting to the business

Support the process with a set of reporting guidelines.

Gather data

IT departments frequently gather large amounts of data, which are not all equally interesting to the business. Start, therefore, by determining the goal and target group of the report and consider how the report is going to be used. Is management going to read it, can managers and department heads consult it online or are you going to present the results at a meeting? And what will be done with it next?

Process and apply data

The business likes to see a hierarchical overview of the performance over the past period. But it is particularly interested in events from the past that may impact, today or in the future, the performance of the business and how the IT department is going to combat those threats.

Present data with cross references to contracted and chargeable service elements. Process these into the language the business understands. Report not only on whether the IT department achieves the SLA arrangements, but indicate also what incidents have occurred and what IT has done to resolve them and to avoid repetition, and what IT is doing to elevate positive exceptions to standard items.

Do not only concentrate on the past but also on the future. This is an excellent marketing opportunity for the IT department in order to clarify the added value to the business. If possible, connect this value directly to the positive or negative experiences of the business.

Publish information

Publish information for the different stakeholders at all levels of the organization and use marketing and communication techniques. Fine-tune the message and method to your target group and its needs from a business perspective. As a rule there are three possible target groups:

- **The business** - wants to know if the IT service provider has delivered the promised services, in SLA terms, and which measures are being taken by the service provider if this is not the case.
- **Senior IT Management** - wants to know if the CSFs and KPIs are attained. It looks at which strategic and tactical improvements are necessary. It needs frequent presentations in the form of a IT Balanced Scorecard.
- **IT Internal** - is interested in KPIs and *metrics,* in order to locate, plan and coordinate improvement potential.

Tune the reporting to the business

Consider by data group if it is valuable for the target group. For example, the business often wants to know *how long* a service was unavailable, since an availability percentage does not provide much insight into its opportunities to use the service. Whether or not the mainframe or the service was available the entire time, is not useful information for the business, but more so the fact that it could not reach the service. Look at this from an *end-to-end* perspective.

Figure 5.6 gives a picture of four different organizational levels and their interests:

1. **strategic thinkers** - want short reports, with lots of attention to the risks, organization image, profitability and cost savings
2. **directors** - want more detailed reports which summarize the development measured in time, indicating how processes support the company goals, and warning of risks
3. **managers and supervisors** - deal with observing the goals, team and process performance, distribution of resources and improvement initiatives. Measurements and reports must indicate how the process results are contributing to this
4. **team leaders and staff** - will look to emphasize the individual contribution to the company result; focus should be to fix individual metrics, acknowledge their skills and consider which training potential is available in order to involve them in the processes

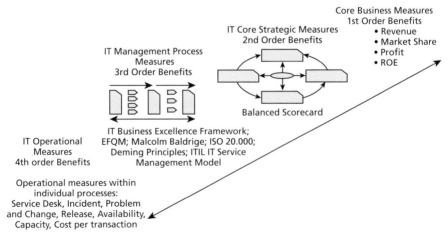

Figure 5.6 Different organizational levels and their needs

Consider the business goals when preparing the presentations. It is only then that IT can answer the question regarding its added value. Besides the negative exceptions, also list the (anticipated) positive results in the presentation.

Use a practical approach: indicate what has happened and what IT has done to resolve it. And in order to prevent a repeat, what IT is doing to elevate positive exceptions to standard practice. A table showing what has been achieved and what has not is not necessarily complicated, see Table 5.1.

Period = > Target	January	February	March	April	May	June	July	August
A								
B								
C								
D								
E								
F								
Legend:								
Goal achieved:								
Goal not achieved:								
Goal threatened:								

Table 5.1 Overview of the Service Level Achievements accomplished

Take the time, together with the business and using the service draft, to make up a business-focused reporting framework: a policy that formulates according to which rules you will be reporting. This should at least contain:
- target groups and their view of the services delivered
- agreement as to what should be measured and what to report
- defining all terms and upper and lower limits
- basis for all calculations
- report planning
- access to reports and media used
- meetings to discuss the reports

Establish this by business Unit. In this way, you can distinguish between the production and sales departments, for example. All reporting, however, must form part of the same reporting framework. Once this has been established, the data can simply be converted into meaningful reports, sometimes even fully automated.

In it, provide clear answers to the core questions, state where the threats and pitfalls lie, where the number of threats has diminished, and what has been improved. Also fine tune the media to the target group: paper reports, online or oral presentation.

Careful and effective automatic reporting is crucial for a successful and continual reporting system that creates value for the business. Evaluate continually whether the existing reporting provides clear and unambiguous information about the performance of the IT department and adjust your reporting, if this is no longer the case.

Acronyms

AMIS	Availability Management Information System
APMG	APM Group
BCM	Business Continuity Management
BCP	Business Continuity Plan
BCS	British Computer Society
BIA	Business Impact Analysis
BPO	Business Process Outsourcing
BU	Business Unit
CAB	Change Advisory Board
CCM	Component Capacity Management
CFIA	Component Failure Impact Analysis
CI	Configuration Item
CMDB	Configuration Management Database
CMIS	Capacity Management Information System
CMS	Configuration Management System
CS	Change Schedule
CSF	Critical Success Factor
CSI	Continual Service Improvement
CSP	Core Service Package
DIKW	Data Information Knowledge Wisdom
DML	Definitive Media Library
ECAB	Emergency Change Advisory Board
ELS	Early Life Support
FTA	Fault Tree Analysis

HR	Human Resources
ISMS	Information Security Management System
ITIL	Information Technology Infrastructure Library
ITSCM	IT Service Continuity Management
itSMF	IT Service Management Forum
KEDB	Known Error Database
KPI	Key Performance Indicator
KPO	Knowledge Process Outsourcing
LCS	Loyalist Certification Services
LOS	Line of Service
M_o_R	Management of Risk
MTBF	Mean Time Between Failures
MTBSI	Mean Time Between Service Incidents
MTTR	Mean Time To Repair
MTRS	Mean Time to Restore Service
OGC	Office of Government Commerce
OLA	Operational Level Agreement
PBA	Pattern of Business Activity
PDCA	Plan Do Check Act
PFS	Prerequisites for Success
PIR	Post-Implementation Review
PRINCE2	PRojects IN Controlled Environments
PSA	Projected Service Availability
PSO	Projected Service Outage
RAD	Rapid Application Development
RFC	Request for Change
SAC	Service Acceptance Criteria
SACM	Service Asset and Configuration Management
SCD	Supplier and Contract Database
SCM	Service Catalogue Management
SDP	Service Design Package
SFA	Service Failure Analysis
SIP	Service Improvement Plan
SKMS	Service Knowledge Management System
SLA	Service Level Agreement
SLM	Service Level Management
SLP	Service Level Package
SLR	Service Level Requirement
SOC	Separation of Concerns

SPM	Service Portfolio Management
SPOC	Single Point of Contact
SPOF	Single Point of Failure
TCU	Total Cost of Utilization
TSO	The Stationary Office
UC	Underpinning Contract
VBF	Vital Business Function
VCD	Variable Cost Dynamics

Glossary

Where a term is relevant to a particular phase in the Lifecycle of an IT Service, or to one of the Core ITIL publications, this is indicated at the beginning of the definition. This glossary is based on the official ITIL V3 Glossary, version 01 of 30 May 2007.

Acceptance	Formal agreement that an IT Service, Process, Plan, or other Deliverable is complete, accurate, Reliable and meets its specified Requirements. Acceptance is usually preceded by Evaluation or Testing and is often required before proceeding to the next stage of a Project or Process. See Service Acceptance Criteria.
Access Management	(Service Operation) The Process responsible for allowing Users to make use of IT Services, data, or other Assets. Access Management helps to protect the Confidentiality, Integrity and Availability of Assets by ensuring that only authorized Users are able to access or modify the Assets. Access Management is sometimes referred to as Rights Management or Identity Management.
Account Manager	(Service Strategy) A Role that is very similar to Business Relationship Manager, but includes more commercial aspects. Most commonly used when dealing with External Customers.
Accounting	(Service Strategy) The Process responsible for identifying actual Costs of delivering IT Services, comparing these with budgeted costs, and managing variance from the Budget.
Accredited	Officially authorized to carry out a Role. For example an Accredited body may be authorized to provide training or to conduct Audits.
Active Monitoring	(Service Operation) Monitoring of a Configuration Item or an IT Service that uses automated regular checks to discover the current status. See Passive Monitoring.

Activity	A set of actions designed to achieve a particular result. Activities are usually defined as part of Processes or Plans, and are documented in Procedures.
Agreed Service Time	(Service Design) A synonym for Service Hours, commonly used in formal calculations of Availability. See Downtime.
Agreement	A Document that describes a formal understanding between two or more parties. An Agreement is not legally binding, unless it forms part of a Contract. See Service Level Agreement, Operational Level Agreement.
Alert	(Service Operation) A warning that a threshold has been reached, something has changed, or a Failure has occurred. Alerts are often created and managed by System Management tools and are managed by the Event Management Process.
Analytical Modeling	(Service Strategy) (Service Design) (Continual Service Improvement) A technique that uses mathematical Models to predict the behavior of a Configuration Item or IT Service. Analytical Models are commonly used in Capacity Management and Availability Management. See Modeling.
Application	Software that provides Functions that are required by an IT Service. Each Application may be part of more than one IT Service. An Application runs on one or more Servers or Clients. See Application Management, Application Portfolio.
Application Management	(Service Design) (Service Operation) The Function responsible for managing Applications throughout their Lifecycle.
Application Portfolio	(Service Design) A database or structured Document used to manage Applications throughout their Lifecycle. The Application Portfolio contains key Attributes of all Applications. The Application Portfolio is sometimes implemented as part of the Service Portfolio, or as part of the Configuration Management System.
Application Service Provider (ASP)	(Service Design) An External Service Provider that provides IT Services using Applications running at the Service Provider's premises. Users access the Applications by network connections to the Service Provider.
Application Sizing	(Service Design) The Activity responsible for understanding the Resource Requirements needed to support a new Application, or a major Change to an existing Application. Application Sizing helps to ensure that the IT Service can meet its agreed Service Level Targets for Capacity and Performance.
Architecture	(Service Design) The structure of a System or IT Service, including the Relationships of Components to each other and to the environment they are in. Architecture also includes the Standards and Guidelines which guide the design and evolution of the System.
Assembly	(Service Transition) A Configuration Item that is made up from a number of other CIs. For example a Server CI may contain CIs for CPUs, Disks, Memory etc.; an IT Service CI may contain many Hardware, Software and other CIs. See Component CI, Build.

Assessment	Inspection and analysis to check whether a Standard or set of Guidelines is being followed, that Records are accurate, or that Efficiency and Effectiveness targets are being met. See Audit.
Asset	(Service Strategy) Any Resource or Capability. Assets of a Service Provider include anything that could contribute to the delivery of a Service. Assets can be one of the following types: Management, Organization, Process, Knowledge, People, Information, Applications, Infrastructure, and Financial Capital.
Asset Management	(Service Transition) Asset Management is the Process responsible for tracking and reporting the value and ownership of financial Assets throughout their Lifecycle. Asset Management is part of an overall Service Asset and Configuration Management Process. See Asset Register.
Asset Register	(Service Transition) A list of Assets, which includes their ownership and value. The Asset Register is maintained by Asset Management.
Attribute	(Service Transition) A piece of information about a Configuration Item. Examples are name, location, Version number, and Cost. Attributes of CIs are recorded in the Configuration Management Database (CMDB). See Relationship.
Audit	Formal inspection and verification to check whether a Standard or set of Guidelines is being followed, that Records are accurate, or that Efficiency and Effectiveness targets are being met. An Audit may be carried out by internal or external groups. See Certification, Assessment.
Authority Matrix	Synonym for RACI.
Automatic Call Distribution (ACD)	(Service Operation) Use of Information Technology to direct an incoming telephone call to the most appropriate person in the shortest possible time. ACD is sometimes called Automated Call Distribution.
Availability	(Service Design) Ability of a Configuration Item or IT Service to perform its agreed Function when required. Availability is determined by Reliability, Maintainability, Serviceability, Performance, and Security. Availability is usually calculated as a percentage. This calculation is often based on Agreed Service Time and Downtime. It is Best Practice to calculate Availability using measurements of the Business output of the IT Service.
Availability Management	(Service Design) The Process responsible for defining, analyzing, Planning, measuring and improving all aspects of the Availability of IT Services. Availability Management is responsible for ensuring that all IT Infrastructure, Processes, Tools, Roles etc are appropriate for the agreed Service Level Targets for Availability.
Availability Management Information System (AMIS)	(Service Design) A virtual repository of all Availability Management data, usually stored in multiple physical locations. See Service Knowledge Management System.

Availability Plan   (Service Design) A Plan to ensure that existing and future Availability Requirements for IT Services can be provided Cost Effectively.

Back-out   Synonym for Remediation.

Backup   (Service Design) (Service Operation) Copying data to protect against loss of Integrity or Availability of the original.

Balanced Scorecard   (Continual Service Improvement) A management tool developed by Drs. Robert Kaplan (Harvard Business School) and David Norton. A Balanced Scorecard enables a Strategy to be broken down into Key Performance Indicators. Performance against the KPIs is used to demonstrate how well the Strategy is being achieved. A Balanced Scorecard has 4 major areas, each of which has a small number of KPIs. The same 4 areas are considered at different levels of detail throughout the Organization.

Baseline   (Continual Service Improvement) A Benchmark used as a reference point. For example:
- An ITSM Baseline can be used as a starting point to measure the effect of a Service Improvement Plan
- A Performance Baseline can be used to measure changes in Performance over the lifetime of an IT Service
- A Configuration Management Baseline can be used to enable the IT Infrastructure to be restored to a known Configuration if a Change or Release fails

Benchmark   (Continual Service Improvement) The recorded state of something at a specific point in time. A Benchmark can be created for a Configuration, a Process, or any other set of data. For example, a benchmark can be used in:
- Continual Service Improvement, to establish the current state for managing improvements.
- Capacity Management, to document Performance characteristics during normal operations.
- See Benchmarking, Baseline.

Benchmarking   (Continual Service Improvement) Comparing a Benchmark with a Baseline or with Best Practice. The term Benchmarking is also used to mean creating a series of Benchmarks over time, and comparing the results to measure progress or improvement.

Best Practice   Proven Activities or Processes that have been successfully used by multiple Organizations. ITIL is an example of Best Practice.

Brainstorming   (Service Design) A technique that helps a team to generate ideas. Ideas are not reviewed during the Brainstorming session, but at a later stage. Brainstorming is often used by Problem Management to identify possible causes.

British Standards Institution (BSI)   The UK National Standards body, responsible for creating and maintaining British Standards. See http://www.bsi-global.com for more information. See ISO.

Budget	A list of all the money an Organization or Business Unit plans to receive, and plans to pay out, over a specified period of time. See Budgeting, Planning.
Budgeting	The Activity of predicting and controlling the spending of money. Consists of a periodic negotiation cycle to set future Budgets (usually annual) and the day-to-day monitoring and adjusting of current Budgets.
Build	(Service Transition) The Activity of assembling a number of Configuration Items to create part of an IT Service. The term Build is also used to refer to a Release that is authorized for distribution. For example Server Build or laptop Build. See Configuration Baseline.
Build Environment	(Service Transition) A controlled Environment where Applications, IT Services and other Builds are assembled prior to being moved into a Test or Live Environment.
Business	(Service Strategy) An overall corporate entity or Organization formed of a number of Business Units. In the context of ITSM, the term Business includes public sector and not-for-profit organizations, as well as companies. An IT Service Provider provides IT Services to a Customer within a Business. The IT Service Provider may be part of the same Business as their Customer (Internal Service Provider), or part of another Business (External Service Provider).
Business Capacity Management (BCM)	(Service Design) In the context of ITSM, Business Capacity Management is the Activity responsible for understanding future Business Requirements for use in the Capacity Plan. See Service Capacity Management.
Business Case	(Service Strategy) Justification for a significant item of expenditure. Includes information about Costs, benefits, options, issues, Risks, and possible problems. See Cost Benefit Analysis.
Business Continuity Management (BCM)	(Service Design) The Business Process responsible for managing Risks that could seriously impact the Business. BCM safeguards the interests of key stakeholders, reputation, brand and value creating activities. The BCM Process involves reducing Risks to an acceptable level and planning for the recovery of Business Processes should a disruption to the Business occur. BCM sets the Objectives, Scope and Requirements for IT Service Continuity Management.
Business Continuity Plan (BCP)	(Service Design) A Plan defining the steps required to Restore Business Processes following a disruption. The Plan will also identify the triggers for Invocation, people to be involved, communications etc. IT Service Continuity Plans form a significant part of Business Continuity Plans.
Business Customer	(Service Strategy) A recipient of a product or a Service from the Business. For example if the Business is a car manufacturer then the Business Customer is someone who buys a car.

Business Impact Analysis (BIA)	(Service Strategy) BIA is the Activity in Business Continuity Management that identifies Vital Business Functions and their dependencies. These dependencies may include Suppliers, people, other Business Processes, IT Services etc. BIA defines the recovery requirements for IT Services. These requirements include Recovery Time Objectives, Recovery Point Objectives and minimum Service Level Targets for each IT Service.
Business Objective	(Service Strategy) The Objective of a Business Process, or of the Business as a whole. Business Objectives support the Business Vision, provide guidance for the IT Strategy, and are often supported by IT Services.
Business Operations	(Service Strategy) The day-to-day execution, monitoring and management of Business Processes.
Business Perspective	(Continual Service Improvement) An understanding of the Service Provider and IT Services from the point of view of the Business, and an understanding of the Business from the point of view of the Service Provider.
Business Process	A Process that is owned and carried out by the Business. A Business Process contributes to the delivery of a product or Service to a Business Customer. For example, a retailer may have a purchasing Process which helps to deliver Services to their Business Customers. Many Business Processes rely on IT Services.
Business Relationship Management	(Service Strategy) The Process or Function responsible for maintaining a Relationship with the Business. BRM usually includes: • Managing personal Relationships with Business managers • Providing input to Service Portfolio Management • Ensuring that the IT Service Provider is satisfying the Business needs of the Customers This Process has strong links with Service Level Management.
Business Relationship Manager (BRM)	(Service Strategy) A Role responsible for maintaining the Relationship with one or more Customers. This Role is often combined with the Service Level Manager Role. See Account Manager.
Business Service	An IT Service that directly supports a Business Process, as opposed to an Infrastructure Service which is used internally by the IT Service Provider and is not usually visible to the Business. The term Business Service is also used to mean a Service that is delivered to Business Customers by Business Units. For example delivery of financial services to Customers of a bank, or goods to the Customers of a retail store. Successful delivery of Business Services often depends on one or more IT Services.
Business Service Management (BSM)	(Service Strategy) (Service Design) An approach to the management of IT Services that considers the Business Processes supported and the Business value provided. This term also means the management of Business Services delivered to Business Customers.
Business Unit	(Service Strategy) A segment of the Business which has its own Plans, Metrics, income and Costs. Each Business Unit owns Assets and uses these to create value for Customers in the form of goods and Services.

Call	(Service Operation) A telephone call to the Service Desk from a User. A Call could result in an Incident or a Service Request being logged.
Call Centre	(Service Operation) An Organization or Business Unit which handles large numbers of incoming and outgoing telephone calls. See Service Desk.
Call Type	(Service Operation) A Category that is used to distinguish incoming requests to a Service Desk. Common Call Types are Incident, Service Request and Complaint.
Capability	(Service Strategy) The ability of an Organization, person, Process, Application, Configuration Item or IT Service to carry out an Activity. Capabilities are intangible Assets of an Organization. See Resource.
Capability Maturity Model (CMM)	(Continual Service Improvement) The Capability Maturity Model for Software (also known as the CMM and SW-CMM) is a model used to identify Best Practices to help increase Process Maturity. CMM was developed at the Software Engineering Institute (SEI) of Carnegie Mellon University. In 2000, the SW-CMM was upgraded to CMMI® (Capability Maturity Model Integration). The SEI no longer maintains the SW-CMM model, its associated appraisal methods, or training materials.
Capability Maturity Model Integration (CMMI)	(Continual Service Improvement) Capability Maturity Model® Integration (CMMI) is a process improvement approach developed by the Software Engineering Institute (SEI) of Carnegie Melon University. CMMI provides organizations with the essential elements of effective processes. It can be used to guide process improvement across a project, a division, or an entire organization. CMMI helps integrate traditionally separate organizational functions, set process improvement goals and priorities, provide guidance for quality processes, and provide a point of reference for appraising current processes. See http://www.sei.cmu.edu/cmmi/ for more information. See CMM, Continuous Improvement, Maturity.
Capacity	(Service Design) The maximum Throughput that a Configuration Item or IT Service can deliver whilst meeting agreed Service Level Targets. For some types of CI, Capacity may be the size or volume, for example a disk drive.
Capacity Management	(Service Design) The Process responsible for ensuring that the Capacity of IT Services and the IT Infrastructure is able to deliver agreed Service Level Targets in a Cost Effective and timely manner. Capacity Management considers all Resources required to deliver the IT Service, and plans for short, medium and long term Business Requirements.
Capacity Management Information System (CMIS)	(Service Design) A virtual repository of all Capacity Management data, usually stored in multiple physical locations. See Service Knowledge Management System.

Capacity Plan	(Service Design) A Capacity Plan is used to manage the Resources required to deliver IT Services. The Plan contains scenarios for different predictions of Business demand, and costed options to deliver the agreed Service Level Targets.
Capacity Planning	(Service Design) The Activity within Capacity Management responsible for creating a Capacity Plan.
Capital Expenditure (CAPEX)	(Service Strategy) The Cost of purchasing something that will become a financial Asset, for example computer equipment and buildings. The value of the Asset is Depreciated over multiple accounting periods.
Capital Item	(Service Strategy) An Asset that is of interest to Financial Management because it is above an agreed financial value.
Capitalization	(Service Strategy) Identifying major Cost as capital, even though no Asset is purchased. This is done to spread the impact of the Cost over multiple accounting periods. The most common example of this is software development, or purchase of a software license.
Category	A named group of things that have something in common. Categories are used to group similar things together. For example Cost Types are used to group similar types of Cost. Incident Categories are used to group similar types of Incident, CI Types are used to group similar types of Configuration Item.
Certification	Issuing a certificate to confirm Compliance to a Standard. Certification includes a formal Audit by an independent and Accredited body. The term Certification is also used to mean awarding a certificate to verify that a person has achieved a qualification.
Change	(Service Transition) The addition, modification or removal of anything that could have an effect on IT Services. The Scope should include all IT Services, Configuration Items, Processes, Documentation etc.
Change Advisory Board (CAB)	(Service Transition) A group of people that advises the Change Manager in the Assessment, prioritization and scheduling of Changes. This board is usually made up of representatives from all areas within the IT Service Provider, the Business, and Third Parties such as Suppliers.
Change Case	(Service Operation) A technique used to predict the impact of proposed Changes. Change Cases use specific scenarios to clarify the scope of proposed Changes and to help with Cost Benefit Analysis. See Use Case.
Change History	(Service Transition) Information about all changes made to a Configuration Item during its life. Change History consists of all those Change Records that apply to the CI.
Change Management	(Service Transition) The Process responsible for controlling the Lifecycle of all Changes. The primary objective of Change Management is to enable beneficial Changes to be made, with minimum disruption to IT Services.

Change Model	(Service Transition) A repeatable way of dealing with a particular Category of Change. A Change Model defines specific pre-defined steps that will be followed for a Change of this Category. Change Models may be very simple, with no requirement for approval (e.g. Password Reset) or may be very complex with many steps that require approval (e.g. major software Release). See Standard Change, Change Advisory Board.
Change Record	(Service Transition) A Record containing the details of a Change. Each Change Record documents the Lifecycle of a single Change. A Change Record is created for every Request for Change that is received, even those that are subsequently rejected. Change Records should reference the Configuration Items that are affected by the Change. Change Records are stored in the Configuration Management System.
Change Request	Synonym for Request for Change.
Change Schedule	(Service Transition) A Document that lists all approved Changes and their planned implementation dates. A Change Schedule is sometimes called a Forward Schedule of Change, even though it also contains information about Changes that have already been implemented.
Change Window	(Service Transition) A regular, agreed time when Changes or Releases may be implemented with minimal impact on Services. Change Windows are usually documented in SLAs.
Charging	(Service Strategy) Requiring payment for IT Services. Charging for IT Services is optional, and many Organizations choose to treat their IT Service Provider as a Cost Centre.
Chronological Analysis	(Service Operation) A technique used to help identify possible causes of Problems. All available data about the Problem is collected and sorted by date and time to provide a detailed timeline. This can make it possible to identify which Events may have been triggered by others.
CI Type	(Service Transition) A Category that is used to Classify CIs. The CI Type identifies the required Attributes and Relationships for a Configuration Record. Common CI Types include: hardware, Document, User etc.
Classification	The act of assigning a Category to something. Classification is used to ensure consistent management and reporting. CIs, Incidents, Problems, Changes etc. are usually classified.
Client	A generic term that means a Customer, the Business or a Business Customer. For example Client Manager may be used as a synonym for Account Manager. The term client is also used to mean: <ul><li>A computer that is used directly by a User, for example a PC, Handheld Computer, or Workstation.</li><li>The part of a Client-Server Application that the User directly interfaces with. For example an email Client.</li></ul>
Closed	(Service Operation) The final Status in the Lifecycle of an Incident, Problem, Change etc. When the Status is Closed, no further action is taken.

Closure	(Service Operation) The act of changing the Status of an Incident, Problem, Change etc. to Closed.
COBIT	(Continual Service Improvement) Control Objectives for Information and related Technology (COBIT) provides guidance and Best Practice for the management of IT Processes. COBIT is published by the IT Governance Institute. See http://www.isaca.org/ for more information.
Code of Practice	A Guideline published by a public body or a Standards Organization, such as ISO or BSI. Many Standards consist of a Code of Practice and a Specification. The Code of Practice describes recommended Best Practice.
Cold Standby	Synonym for Gradual Recovery.
Commercial off the Shelf (COTS)	(Service Design) Application software or Middleware that can be purchased from a Third Party.
Compliance	Ensuring that a Standard or set of Guidelines is followed, or that proper, consistent accounting or other practices are being employed.
Component	A general term that is used to mean one part of something more complex. For example, a computer System may be a component of an IT Service, an Application may be a Component of a Release Unit. Components that need to be managed should be Configuration Items.
Component Capacity Management (CCM)	(Service Design) (Continual Service Improvement) The Process responsible for understanding the Capacity, Utilization, and Performance of Configuration Items. Data is collected, recorded and analyzed for use in the Capacity Plan. See Service Capacity Management.
Component CI	(Service Transition) A Configuration Item that is part of an Assembly. For example, a CPU or Memory CI may be part of a Server CI.
Component Failure Impact Analysis (CFIA)	(Service Design) A technique that helps to identify the impact of CI failure on IT Services. A matrix is created with IT Services on one edge and CIs on the other. This enables the identification of critical CIs (that could cause the failure of multiple IT Services) and of fragile IT Services (that have multiple Single Points of Failure).
Computer Telephony Integration (CTI)	(Service Operation) CTI is a general term covering any kind of integration between computers and telephone Systems. It is most commonly used to refer to Systems where an Application displays detailed screens relating to incoming or outgoing telephone calls. See Automatic Call Distribution, Interactive Voice Response.
Concurrency	A measure of the number of Users engaged in the same Operation at the same time.
Confidentiality	(Service Design) A security principle that requires that data should only be accessed by authorized people.

Configuration	(Service Transition) A generic term, used to describe a group of Configuration Items that work together to deliver an IT Service, or a recognizable part of an IT Service. Configuration is also used to describe the parameter settings for one or more CIs.
Configuration Baseline	(Service Transition) A Baseline of a Configuration that has been formally agreed and is managed through the Change Management process. A Configuration Baseline is used as a basis for future Builds, Releases and Changes.
Configuration Control	(Service Transition) The Activity responsible for ensuring that adding, modifying or removing a CI is properly managed, for example by submitting a Request for Change or Service Request.
Configuration Identification	(Service Transition) The Activity responsible for collecting information about Configuration Items and their Relationships, and loading this information into the CMDB. Configuration Identification is also responsible for labeling the CIs themselves, so that the corresponding Configuration Records can be found.
Configuration Item (CI)	(Service Transition) Any Component that needs to be managed in order to deliver an IT Service. Information about each CI is recorded in a Configuration Record within the Configuration Management System and is maintained throughout its Lifecycle by Configuration Management. CIs are under the control of Change Management. CIs typically include IT Services, hardware, software, buildings, people, and formal documentation such as Process documentation and SLAs.
Configuration Management	(Service Transition) The Process responsible for maintaining information about Configuration Items required to deliver an IT Service, including their Relationships. This information is managed throughout the Lifecycle of the CI. Configuration Management is part of an overall Service Asset and Configuration Management Process.
Configuration Management Database (CMDB)	(Service Transition) A database used to store Configuration Records throughout their Lifecycle. The Configuration Management System maintains one or more CMDBs, and each CMDB stores Attributes of CIs, and Relationships with other CIs.
Configuration Management System (CMS)	(Service Transition) A set of tools and databases that are used to manage an IT Service Provider's Configuration data. The CMS also includes information about Incidents, Problems, Known Errors, Changes and Releases; and may contain data about employees, Suppliers, locations, Business Units, Customers and Users. The CMS includes tools for collecting, storing, managing, updating, and presenting data about all Configuration Items and their Relationships. The CMS is maintained by Configuration Management and is used by all IT Service Management Processes. See Configuration Management Database, Service Knowledge Management System.
Configuration Record	(Service Transition) A Record containing the details of a Configuration Item. Each Configuration Record documents the Lifecycle of a single CI. Configuration Records are stored in a Configuration Management Database.

Configuration Structure	(Service Transition) The hierarchy and other Relationships between all the Configuration Items that comprise a Configuration.
Continual Service Improvement (CSI)	(Continual Service Improvement) A stage in the Lifecycle of an IT Service and the title of one of the Core ITIL publications. Continual Service Improvement is responsible for managing improvements to IT Service Management Processes and IT Services. The Performance of the IT Service Provider is continually measured and improvements are made to Processes, IT Services and IT Infrastructure in order to increase Efficiency, Effectiveness, and Cost Effectiveness. See Plan-Do-Check-Act.
Continuous Availability	(Service Design) An approach or design to achieve 100% Availability. A Continuously Available IT Service has no planned or unplanned Downtime.
Continuous Operation	(Service Design) An approach or design to eliminate planned Downtime of an IT Service. Note that individual Configuration Items may be down even though the IT Service is Available.
Contract	A legally binding Agreement between two or more parties.
Contract Portfolio	(Service Strategy) A database or structured Document used to manage Service Contracts or Agreements between an IT Service Provider and their Customers. Each IT Service delivered to a Customer should have a Contract or other Agreement which is listed in the Contract Portfolio. See Service Portfolio, Service Catalogue.
Control	A means of managing a Risk, ensuring that a Business Objective is achieved, or ensuring that a Process is followed. Example Controls include Policies, Procedures, Roles, RAID, door-locks etc. A control is sometimes called a Countermeasure or safeguard. Control also means to manage the utilization or behavior of a Configuration Item, System or IT Service.
Control Objectives for Information and related Technology (CobiT)	See CobiT.
Control perspective	(Service Strategy) An approach to the management of IT Services, Processes, Functions, Assets etc. There can be several different Control Perspectives on the same IT Service, Process etc., allowing different individuals or teams to focus on what is important and relevant to their specific Role. Example Control Perspectives include Reactive and Proactive management within IT Operations, or a Lifecycle view for an Application Project team.
Control Processes	The ISO/IEC 20000 Process group that includes Change Management and Configuration Management.

Core Service	(Service Strategy) An IT Service that delivers basic Outcomes desired by one or more Customers. See Supporting Service, Core Service Package.
Core Service Package (CSP)	(Service Strategy) A detailed description of a Core Service that may be shared by two or more Service Level Packages. See Service Package.
Cost	The amount of money spent on a specific Activity, IT Service, or Business Unit. Costs consist of real cost (money), notional cost such as people's time, and Depreciation.
Cost Benefit Analysis	An Activity that analyses and compares the Costs and the benefits involved in one or more alternative courses of action. See Business Case, Net Present Value, Internal Rate of Return, Return on Investment, Value on Investment.
Cost Centre	(Service Strategy) A Business Unit or Project to which Costs are assigned. A Cost Centre does not charge for Services provided. An IT Service Provider can be run as a Cost Centre or a Profit Centre.
Cost Effectiveness	A measure of the balance between the Effectiveness and Cost of a Service, Process or activity, A Cost Effective Process is one which achieves its Objectives at minimum Cost. See KPI, Return on Investment, Value for Money.
Cost Element	(Service Strategy) The middle level of category to which Costs are assigned in Budgeting and Accounting. The highest level category is Cost Type. For example a Cost Type of "people" could have cost elements of payroll, staff benefits, expenses, training, overtime etc. Cost Elements can be further broken down to give Cost Units. For example the Cost Element "expenses" could include Cost Units of Hotels, Transport, Meals etc.
Cost Management	(Service Strategy) A general term that is used to refer to Budgeting and Accounting, sometimes used as a synonym for Financial Management
Cost Type	(Service Strategy) The highest level of category to which Costs are assigned in Budgeting and Accounting. For example hardware, software, people, accommodation, external and Transfer. See Cost Element, Cost Type.
Cost Unit	(Service Strategy) The lowest level of category to which Costs are assigned, Cost Units are usually things that can be easily counted (e.g. staff numbers, software licenses) or things easily measured (e.g. CPU usage, Electricity consumed). Cost Units are included within Cost Elements. For example a Cost Element of "expenses" could include Cost Units of Hotels, Transport, Meals etc. See Cost Type.

Countermeasure	Can be used to refer to any type of Control. The term Countermeasure is most often used when referring to measures that increase Resilience, Fault Tolerance or Reliability of an IT Service.
Course Corrections	Changes made to a Plan or Activity that has already started, to ensure that it will meet its Objectives. Course corrections are made as a result of Monitoring progress.
CRAMM	A methodology and tool for analyzing and managing Risks. CRAMM was developed by the UK Government, but is now privately owned. Further information is available from http://www.cramm.com/
Crisis Management	The Process responsible for managing the wider implications of Business Continuity. A Crisis Management team is responsible for Strategic issues such as managing media relations and shareholder confidence, and decides when to invoke Business Continuity Plans.
Critical Success Factor (CSF)	Something that must happen if a Process, Project, Plan, or IT Service is to succeed. KPIs are used to measure the achievement of each CSF. For example a CSF of "protect IT Services when making Changes" could be measured by KPIs such as "percentage reduction of unsuccessful Changes", "percentage reduction in Changes causing Incidents" etc.
Culture	A set of values that is shared by a group of people, including expectations about how people should behave, ideas, beliefs, and practices. See Vision.
Customer	Someone who buys goods or Services. The Customer of an IT Service Provider is the person or group who defines and agrees the Service Level Targets. The term Customers is also sometimes informally used to mean Users, for example "this is a Customer focused Organization".
Customer Portfolio	(Service Strategy) A database or structured Document used to record all Customers of the IT Service Provider. The Customer Portfolio is the Business Relationship Manager's view of the Customers who receive Services from the IT Service Provider. See Contract Portfolio, Service Portfolio.
Dashboard	(Service Operation) A graphical representation of overall IT Service Performance and Availability. Dashboard images may be updated in real-time, and can also be included in management reports and web pages. Dashboards can be used to support Service Level Management, Event Management or Incident Diagnosis.
Data-to-Information-to-Knowledge-to-Wisdom (DIKW)	A way of understanding the relationships between data, information, knowledge, and wisdom. DIKW shows how each of these builds on the others.

Definitive Media Library (DML)	(Service Transition) One or more locations in which the definitive and approved versions of all software Configuration Items are securely stored. The DML may also contain associated CIs such as licenses and documentation. The DML is a single logical storage area even if there are multiple locations. All software in the DML is under the control of Change and Release Management and is recorded in the Configuration Management System. Only software from the DML is acceptable for use in a Release.
Deliverable	Something that must be provided to meet a commitment in a Service Level Agreement or a Contract. Deliverable is also used in a more informal way to mean a planned output of any Process.
Demand Management	Activities that understand and influence Customer demand for Services and the provision of Capacity to meet these demands. At a Strategic level Demand Management can involve analysis of Patterns of Business Activity and User Profiles. At a Tactical level it can involve use of Differential Charging to encourage Customers to use IT Services at less busy times. See Capacity Management.
Deming Cycle	Synonym for Plan Do Check Act.
Dependency	The direct or indirect reliance of one Process or Activity upon another.
Deployment	(Service Transition) The Activity responsible for movement of new or changed hardware, software, documentation, Process, etc to the Live Environment. Deployment is part of the Release and Deployment Management Process. See Rollout.
Depreciation	(Service Strategy) A measure of the reduction in value of an Asset over its life. This is based on wearing out, consumption or other reduction in the useful economic value.
Design	(Service Design) An Activity or Process that identifies Requirements and then defines a solution that is able to meet these Requirements. See Service Design.
Detection	(Service Operation) A stage in the Incident Lifecycle. Detection results in the Incident becoming known to the Service Provider. Detection can be automatic, or can be the result of a User logging an Incident.
Development	(Service Design) The Process responsible for creating or modifying an IT Service or Application. Also used to mean the Role or group that carries out Development work.
Development Environment	(Service Design) An Environment used to create or modify IT Services or Applications. Development Environments are not typically subjected to the same degree of control as Test Environments or Live Environments. See Development.

Diagnosis	(Service Operation) A stage in the Incident and Problem Lifecycles. The purpose of Diagnosis is to identify a Workaround for an Incident or the Root Cause of a Problem.
Diagnostic Script	(Service Operation) A structured set of questions used by Service Desk staff to ensure they ask the correct questions, and to help them Classify, Resolve and assign Incidents. Diagnostic Scripts may also be made available to Users to help them diagnose and resolve their own Incidents.
Differential Charging	A technique used to support Demand Management by charging different amounts for the same IT Service Function at different times.
Direct Cost	(Service Strategy) A cost of providing an IT Service which can be allocated in full to a specific Customer, Cost Centre, Project etc. For example cost of providing non-shared servers or software licenses. See Indirect Cost.
Directory Service	(Service Operation) An Application that manages information about IT Infrastructure available on a network, and corresponding User access Rights.
Do Nothing	(Service Design) A Recovery Option. The Service Provider formally agrees with the Customer that Recovery of this IT Service will not be performed.
Document	Information in readable form. A Document may be paper or electronic. For example a Policy statement, Service Level Agreement, Incident Record, diagram of computer room layout. See Record.
Downtime	(Service Design) (Service Operation) The time when a Configuration Item or IT Service is not Available during its Agreed Service Time. The Availability of an IT Service is often calculated from Agreed Service Time and Downtime.
Driver	Something that influences Strategy, Objectives or Requirements. For example new legislation or the actions of competitors.
Early Life Support	(Service Transition) Support provided for a new or Changed IT Service for a period of time after it is Released. During Early Life Support the IT Service Provider may review the KPIs, Service Levels and Monitoring Thresholds, and provide additional Resources for Incident and Problem Management.
Economies of scale	(Service Strategy) The reduction in average Cost that is possible from increasing the usage of an IT Service or Asset. See Economies of Scope.
Economies of scope	(Service Strategy) The reduction in Cost that is allocated to an IT Service by using an existing Asset for an additional purpose. For example delivering a new IT Service from existing IT Infrastructure. See Economies of Scale.

Effectiveness	(Continual Service Improvement) A measure of whether the Objectives of a Process, Service or Activity have been achieved. An Effective Process or Activity is one that achieves its agreed Objectives. See KPI.
Efficiency	(Continual Service Improvement) A measure of whether the right amount of resources have been used to deliver a Process, Service or Activity. An Efficient Process achieves its Objectives with the minimum amount of time, money, people or other resources. See KPI.
Emergency Change	(Service Transition) A Change that must be introduced as soon as possible. For example to resolve a Major Incident or implement a Security patch. The Change Management Process will normally have a specific Procedure for handling Emergency Changes. See Emergency Change Advisory Board (ECAB).
Emergency Change Advisory Board (ECAB)	(Service Transition) A sub-set of the Change Advisory Board who make decisions about high impact Emergency Changes. Membership of the ECAB may be decided at the time a meeting is called, and depends on the nature of the Emergency Change.
Environment	(Service Transition) A subset of the IT Infrastructure that is used for a particular purpose. For Example: Live Environment, Test Environment, Build Environment. It is possible for multiple Environments to share a Configuration Item, for example Test and Live Environments may use different partitions on a single mainframe computer. Also used in the term Physical Environment to mean the accommodation, air conditioning, power system etc. Environment is also used as a generic term to mean the external conditions that influence or affect something.
Error	(Service Operation) A design flaw or malfunction that causes a Failure of one or more Configuration Items or IT Services. A mistake made by a person or a faulty Process that impacts a CI or IT Service is also an Error.
Escalation	(Service Operation) An Activity that obtains additional Resources when these are needed to meet Service Level Targets or Customer expectations. Escalation may be needed within any IT Service Management Process, but is most commonly associated with Incident Management, Problem Management and the management of Customer complaints. There are two types of Escalation, Functional Escalation and Hierarchic Escalation.
eSourcing Capability Model for Client Organizations (eSCM-CL)	(Service Strategy) A framework to help Organizations guide their analysis and decisions on Service Sourcing Models and Strategies. eSCM-CL was developed by Carnegie Mellon University. See eSCM-SP.

eSourcing Capability Model for Service Providers (eSCM-SP)	(Service Strategy) A framework to help IT Service Providers develop their IT Service Management Capabilities from a Service Sourcing perspective. eSCM-SP was developed by Carnegie Mellon University. See eSCM-CL.
Estimation	The use of experience to provide an approximate value for a Metric or Cost. Estimation is also used in Capacity and Availability Management as the cheapest and least accurate Modeling method.
Evaluation	(Service Transition) The Process responsible for assessing a new or Changed IT Service to ensure that Risks have been managed and to help determine whether to proceed with the Change. Evaluation is also used to mean comparing an actual Outcome with the intended Outcome, or comparing one alternative with another.
Event	(Service Operation) A change of state which has significance for the management of a Configuration Item or IT Service. The term Event is also used to mean an Alert or notification created by any IT Service, Configuration Item or Monitoring tool. Events typically require IT Operations personnel to take actions, and often lead to Incidents being logged.
Event Management	(Service Operation) The Process responsible for managing Events throughout their Lifecycle. Event Management is one of the main Activities of IT Operations.
Exception Report	A Document containing details of one or more KPIs or other important targets that have exceeded defined Thresholds. Examples include SLA targets being missed or about to be missed, and a Performance Metric indicating a potential Capacity problem.
Expanded Incident Lifecycle	(Availability Management) Detailed stages in the Lifecycle of an Incident. The stages are Detection, Diagnosis, Repair, Recovery, Restoration. The Expanded Incident Lifecycle is used to help understand all contributions to the Impact of Incidents and to Plan how these could be controlled or reduced.
External Customer	A Customer who works for a different Business to the IT Service Provider. See External Service Provider, Internal Customer.
External Metric	A Metric that is used to measure the delivery of IT Service to a Customer. External Metrics are usually defined in SLAs and reported to Customers. See Internal Metric.
External Service Provider	(Service Strategy) An IT Service Provider which is part of a different Organization to their Customer. An IT Service Provider may have both Internal Customers and External Customers. See Type III Service Provider.
External Sourcing	Synonym for Outsourcing.

Facilities Management	(Service Operation) The Function responsible for managing the physical Environment where the IT Infrastructure is located. Facilities Management includes all aspects of managing the physical Environment, for example power and cooling, building Access Management, and environmental Monitoring.
Failure	(Service Operation) Loss of ability to Operate to Specification, or to deliver the required output. The term Failure may be used when referring to IT Services, Processes, Activities, Configuration Items etc. A Failure often causes an Incident.
Failure Modes and Effects Analysis (FMEA)	An approach to assessing the potential Impact of Failures. FMEA involves analyzing what would happen after Failure of each Configuration Item, all the way up to the effect on the Business. FMEA is often used in Information Security Management and in IT Service Continuity Planning.
Fast Recovery	(Service Design) A Recovery Option which is also known as Hot Standby. Provision is made to Recover the IT Service in a short period of time, typically less than 24 hours. Fast Recovery typically uses a dedicated Fixed Facility with computer Systems, and software configured ready to run the IT Services. Immediate Recovery may take up to 24 hours if there is a need to Restore data from Backups.
Fault	Synonym for Error.
Fault Tolerance	(Service Design) The ability of an IT Service or Configuration Item to continue to Operate correctly after Failure of a Component part. See Resilience, Countermeasure.
Fault Tree Analysis (FTA)	(Service Design) (Continual Service Improvement) A technique that can be used to determine the chain of Events that leads to a Problem. Fault Tree Analysis represents a chain of Events using Boolean notation in a diagram.
Financial Management	(Service Strategy) The Function and Processes responsible for managing an IT Service Provider's Budgeting, Accounting and Charging Requirements.
First-line Support	(Service Operation) The first level in a hierarchy of Support Groups involved in the resolution of Incidents. Each level contains more specialist skills, or has more time or other Resources. See Escalation.
Fishbone Diagram	Synonym for Ishikawa Diagram.
Fit for Purpose	An informal term used to describe a Process, Configuration Item, IT Service etc. that is capable of meeting its Objectives or Service Levels. Being Fit for Purpose requires suitable Design, implementation, Control and maintenance.
Fixed Cost	(Service Strategy) A Cost that does not vary with IT Service usage. For example the cost of Server hardware. See Variable Cost.

Fixed Facility

(Service Design) A permanent building, available for use when needed by an IT Service Continuity Plan.
See Recovery Option, Portable Facility.

Follow the Sun

(Service Operation) A methodology for using Service Desks and Support Groups around the world to provide seamless 24 * 7 Service. Calls, Incidents, Problems and Service Requests are passed between groups in different time zones.

Fulfilment

Performing Activities to meet a need or Requirement. For example by providing a new IT Service, or meeting a Service Request.

Function

A team or group of people and the tools they use to carry out one or more Processes or Activities. For example the Service Desk.
The term Function also has two other meanings

- An intended purpose of a Configuration Item, Person, Team, Process, or IT Service. For example one Function of an Email Service may be to store and forward outgoing mails, one Function of a Business Process may be to dispatch goods to Customers.
- To perform the intended purpose correctly, "The computer is Functioning"

Functional Escalation

(Service Operation) Transferring an Incident, Problem or Change to a technical team with a higher level of expertise to assist in an Escalation.

Gap Analysis

(Continual Service Improvement) An Activity which compares two sets of data and identifies the differences. Gap Analysis is commonly used to compare a set of Requirements with actual delivery.
See Benchmarking.

Governance

Ensuring that Policies and Strategy are actually implemented, and that required Processes are correctly followed. Governance includes defining Roles and responsibilities, measuring and reporting, and taking actions to resolve any issues identified.

Gradual Recovery

(Service Design) A Recovery Option which is also known as Cold Standby. Provision is made to Recover the IT Service in a period of time greater than 72 hours. Gradual Recovery typically uses a Portable or Fixed Facility that has environmental support and network cabling, but no computer Systems. The hardware and software are installed as part of the IT Service Continuity Plan.

Guideline

A Document describing Best Practice, that recommends what should be done. Compliance to a guideline is not normally enforced.
See Standard.

Help Desk

(Service Operation) A point of contact for Users to log Incidents. A Help Desk is usually more technically focused than a Service Desk and does not provide a Single Point of Contact for all interaction. The term Help Desk is often used as a synonym for Service Desk.

Hierarchic Escalation

(Service Operation) Informing or involving more senior levels of management to assist in an Escalation.

High Availability	(Service Design) An approach or Design that minimizes or hides the effects of Configuration Item Failure on the Users of an IT Service. High Availability solutions are Designed to achieve an agreed level of Availability and make use of techniques such as Fault Tolerance, Resilience and fast Recovery to reduce the number of Incidents, and the Impact of Incidents.
Hot Standby	Synonym for Fast Recovery or Immediate Recovery.
Identity	(Service Operation) A unique name that is used to identify a User, person or Role. The Identity is used to grant Rights to that User, person, or Role. Example identities might be the username SmithJ or the Role "Change manager".
Immediate Recovery	(Service Design) A Recovery Option which is also known as Hot Standby. Provision is made to Recover the IT Service with no loss of Service. Immediate Recovery typically uses mirroring, load balancing and split site technologies.
Impact	(Service Operation) (Service Transition) A measure of the effect of an Incident, Problem or Change on Business Processes. Impact is often based on how Service Levels will be affected. Impact and Urgency are used to assign Priority.
Incident	(Service Operation) An unplanned interruption to an IT Service or a reduction in the Quality of an IT Service. Failure of a Configuration Item that has not yet impacted Service is also an Incident. For example Failure of one disk from a mirror set.
Incident Management	(Service Operation) The Process responsible for managing the Lifecycle of all Incidents. The primary Objective of Incident Management is to return the IT Service to Users as quickly as possible.
Incident Record	(Service Operation) A Record containing the details of an Incident. Each Incident record documents the Lifecycle of a single Incident.
Indirect Cost	(Service Strategy) A Cost of providing an IT Service which cannot be allocated in full to a specific Customer. For example Cost of providing shared Servers or software licenses. Also known as Overhead. See Direct Cost.
Information Security Management (ISM)	(Service Design) The Process that ensures the Confidentiality, Integrity and Availability of an Organization's Assets, information, data and IT Services. Information Security Management usually forms part of an Organizational approach to Security Management which has a wider scope than the IT Service Provider, and includes handling of paper, building access, phone calls etc., for the entire Organization.
Information Security Management System (ISMS)	(Service Design) The framework of Policy, Processes, Standards, Guidelines and tools that ensures an Organization can achieve its Information Security Management Objectives.
Information Security Policy	(Service Design) The Policy that governs the Organization's approach to Information Security Management.

Information   The use of technology for the storage, communication or processing of
Technology (IT)   information. The technology typically includes computers, telecommunications,
                         Applications and other software. The information may include Business data,
                         voice, images, video, etc. Information Technology is often used to support Business
                         Processes through IT Services.

Infrastructure Service   An IT Service that is not directly used by the Business, but is required by the IT
                         Service Provider so they can provide other IT Services. For example Directory
                         Services, naming services, or communication services.

Insourcing   Synonym for Internal Sourcing.

Integrity   (Service Design) A security principle that ensures data and Configuration Items
                         are only modified by authorized personnel and Activities. Integrity considers
                         all possible causes of modification, including software and hardware Failure,
                         environmental Events, and human intervention.

Interactive Voice   (Service Operation) A form of Automatic Call Distribution that accepts User input,
Response (IVR)   such as key presses and spoken commands, to identify the correct destination for
                         incoming Calls.

Intermediate   (Service Design) A Recovery Option which is also known as Warm Standby.
Recovery   Provision is made to Recover the IT Service in a period of time between 24 and 72
                         hours. Intermediate Recovery typically uses a shared Portable or Fixed Facility that
                         has computer Systems and network Components. The hardware and software will
                         need to be configured, and data will need to be restored, as part of the IT Service
                         Continuity Plan.

Internal Customer   A Customer who works for the same Business as the IT Service Provider.
                         See Internal Service Provider, External Customer.

Internal Metric   A Metric that is used within the IT Service Provider to Monitor the Efficiency,
                         Effectiveness or Cost Effectiveness of the IT Service Provider's internal Processes.
                         Internal Metrics are not normally reported to the Customer of the IT Service. See
                         External Metric.

Internal Rate of   (Service Strategy) A technique used to help make decisions about Capital
Return (IRR)   Expenditure. IRR calculates a figure that allows two or more alternative investments
                         to be compared. A larger IRR indicates a better investment.
                         See Net Present Value, Return on Investment.

Internal Service   (Service Strategy) An IT Service Provider which is part of the same Organization
Provider   as their Customer. An IT Service Provider may have both Internal Customers and
                         External Customers.
                         See Type I Service Provider, Type II Service Provider, Insource.

Internal Sourcing   (Service Strategy) Using an Internal Service Provider to manage IT Services.
                         See Service Sourcing, Type I Service Provider, Type II Service Provider.

International Organization for Standardization (ISO)	The International Organization for Standardization (ISO) is the world's largest developer of Standards. ISO is a non-governmental organization which is a network of the national standards institutes of 156 countries. Further information about ISO is available from http://www.iso.org/
International Standards Organization	See International Organization for Standardization (ISO)
Internet Service Provider (ISP)	An External Service Provider that provides access to the Internet. Most ISPs also provide other IT Services such as web hosting.
Invocation	(Service Design) Initiation of the steps defined in a plan. For example initiating the IT Service Continuity Plan for one or more IT Services.
Ishikawa Diagram	(Service Operation) (Continual Service Improvement) A technique that helps a team to identify all the possible causes of a Problem. Originally devised by Kaoru Ishikawa, the output of this technique is a diagram that looks like a fishbone.
ISO 9000	A generic term that refers to a number of international Standards and Guidelines for Quality Management Systems. See http://www.iso.org/ for more information. See ISO.
ISO 9001	An international Standard for Quality Management Systems. See ISO 9000, Standard.
ISO/IEC 17799	(Continual Service Improvement) ISO Code of Practice for Information Security Management. See Standard.
ISO/IEC 20000	ISO Specification and Code of Practice for IT Service Management. ISO/IEC 20000 is aligned with ITIL Best Practice.
ISO/IEC 27001	(Service Design) (Continual Service Improvement) ISO Specification for Information Security Management. The corresponding Code of Practice is ISO/IEC 17799. See Standard.
IT Directorate	(Continual Service Improvement) Senior Management within a Service Provider, charged with developing and delivering IT services. Most commonly used in UK Government departments.
IT Infrastructure	All of the hardware, software, networks, facilities etc. that are required to Develop, Test, deliver, Monitor, Control or support IT Services. The term IT Infrastructure includes all of the Information Technology but not the associated people, Processes and documentation.
IT Operations	(Service Operation) Activities carried out by IT Operations Control, including Console Management, Job Scheduling, Backup and Restore, and Print and Output Management. IT Operations is also used as a synonym for Service Operation.

IT Operations Control	(Service Operation) The Function responsible for Monitoring and Control of the IT Services and IT Infrastructure. See Operations Bridge.
IT Operations Management	(Service Operation) The Function within an IT Service Provider which performs the daily Activities needed to manage IT Services and the supporting IT Infrastructure. IT Operations Management includes IT Operations Control and Facilities Management.
IT Service	A Service provided to one or more Customers by an IT Service Provider. An IT Service is based on the use of Information Technology and supports the Customer's Business Processes. An IT Service is made up from a combination of people, Processes and technology and should be defined in a Service Level Agreement.
IT Service Continuity Management (ITSCM)	(Service Design) The Process responsible for managing Risks that could seriously impact IT Services. ITSCM ensures that the IT Service Provider can always provide minimum agreed Service Levels, by reducing the Risk to an acceptable level and Planning for the Recovery of IT Services. ITSCM should be designed to support Business Continuity Management.
IT Service Continuity Plan	(Service Design) A Plan defining the steps required to Recover one or more IT Services. The Plan will also identify the triggers for Invocation, people to be involved, communications etc. The IT Service Continuity Plan should be part of a Business Continuity Plan.
IT Service Management (ITSM)	The implementation and management of Quality IT Services that meet the needs of the Business. IT Service Management is performed by IT Service Providers through an appropriate mix of people, Process and Information Technology. See Service Management.
IT Service Management Forum (itSMF)	The IT Service Management Forum is an independent Organization dedicated to promoting a professional approach to IT Service Management. The itSMF is a not-for-profit membership Organization with representation in many countries around the world (itSMF Chapters). The itSMF and its membership contribute to the development of ITIL and associated IT Service Management Standards. See http://www.itsmf.com/ for more information.
IT Service Provider	(Service Strategy) A Service Provider that provides IT Services to Internal Customers or External Customers.
IT Steering Group (ISG)	A formal group that is responsible for ensuring that Business and IT Service Provider Strategies and Plans are closely aligned. An IT Steering Group includes senior representatives from the Business and the IT Service Provider.
ITIL	A set of Best Practice guidance for IT Service Management. ITIL is owned by the OGC and consists of a series of publications giving guidance on the provision of Quality IT Services, and on the Processes and facilities needed to support them. See http://www.itil.co.uk/ for more information.

Job Description	A Document which defines the Roles, responsibilities, skills and knowledge required by a particular person. One Job Description can include multiple Roles, for example the Roles of Configuration Manager and Change Manager may be carried out by one person.
Job Scheduling	(Service Operation) Planning and managing the execution of software tasks that are required as part of an IT Service. Job Scheduling is carried out by IT Operations Management, and is often automated using software tools that run batch or online tasks at specific times of the day, week, month or year.
Kano Model	(Service Strategy) A Model developed by Noriaki Kano that is used to help understand Customer preferences. The Kano Model considers Attributes of an IT Service grouped into areas such as Basic Factors, Excitement Factors, Performance Factors etc.
Kepner & Tregoe Analysis	(Service Operation) (Continual Service Improvement) A structured approach to Problem solving. The Problem is analyzed in terms of what, where, when and extent. Possible causes are identified. The most probable cause is tested. The true cause is verified.
Key Performance Indicator (KPI)	(Continual Service Improvement) A Metric that is used to help manage a Process, IT Service or Activity. Many Metrics may be measured, but only the most important of these are defined as KPIs and used to actively manage and report on the Process, IT Service or Activity. KPIs should be selected to ensure that Efficiency, Effectiveness, and Cost Effectiveness are all managed. See Critical Success Factor.
Knowledge Base	(Service Transition) A logical database containing the data used by the Service Knowledge Management System.
Knowledge Management	(Service Transition) The Process responsible for gathering, analyzing, storing and sharing knowledge and information within an Organization. The primary purpose of Knowledge Management is to improve Efficiency by reducing the need to rediscover knowledge. See Data-to-Information-to-Knowledge-to-Wisdom, Service Knowledge Management System.
Known Error	(Service Operation) A Problem that has a documented Root Cause and a Workaround. Known Errors are created and managed throughout their Lifecycle by Problem Management. Known Errors may also be identified by Development or Suppliers.
Known Error Database (KEDB)	(Service Operation) A database containing all Known Error Records. This database is created by Problem Management and used by Incident and Problem Management. The Known Error Database is part of the Service Knowledge Management System.
Known Error Record	(Service Operation) A Record containing the details of a Known Error. Each Known Error Record documents the Lifecycle of a Known Error, including the Status, Root Cause and Workaround. In some implementations a Known Error is documented using additional fields in a Problem Record.

Lifecycle	The various stages in the life of an IT Service, Configuration Item, Incident, Problem, Change etc. The Lifecycle defines the Categories for Status and the Status transitions that are permitted. For example:

- The Lifecycle of an Application includes Requirements, Design, Build, Deploy, Operate, Optimize.
- The Expanded Incident Lifecycle includes Detect, Respond, Diagnose, Repair, Recover, Restore.
- The lifecycle of a Server may include: Ordered, Received, In Test, Live, Disposed etc.

Line of Service (LOS)	(Service Strategy) A Core Service or Supporting Service that has multiple Service Level Packages. A line of Service is managed by a Product Manager and each Service Level Package is designed to support a particular market segment.
Live	(Service Transition) Refers to an IT Service or Configuration Item that is being used to deliver Service to a Customer.
Live Environment	(Service Transition) A controlled Environment containing Live Configuration Items used to deliver IT Services to Customers.
Maintainability	(Service Design) A measure of how quickly and Effectively a Configuration Item or IT Service can be restored to normal working after a Failure. Maintainability is often measured and reported as MTRS. Maintainability is also used in the context of Software or IT Service Development to mean ability to be Changed or Repaired easily.
Major Incident	(Service Operation) The highest Category of Impact for an Incident. A Major Incident results in significant disruption to the Business.
Managed Services	(Service Strategy) A perspective on IT Services which emphasizes the fact that they are managed. The term Managed Services is also used as a synonym for Outsourced IT Services.
Management Information	Information that is used to support decision making by managers. Management Information is often generated automatically by tools supporting the various IT Service Management Processes. Management Information often includes the values of KPIs such as "Percentage of Changes leading to Incidents", or "first time fix rate".
Management of Risk (MoR)	The OGC methodology for managing Risks. MoR includes all the Activities required to identify and Control the exposure to Risk which may have an impact on the achievement of an Organization's Business Objectives. See http://www.m-o-r.org/ for more details.
Management System	The framework of Policy, Processes and Functions that ensures an Organization can achieve its Objectives.
Manual Workaround	A Workaround that requires manual intervention. Manual Workaround is also used as the name of a Recovery Option in which The Business Process Operates without the use of IT Services. This is a temporary measure and is usually combined with another Recovery Option.

Marginal Cost	(Service Strategy) The Cost of continuing to provide the IT Service. Marginal Cost does not include investment already made, for example the cost of developing new software and delivering training.
Market Space	(Service Strategy) All opportunities that an IT Service Provider could exploit to meet business needs of Customers. The Market Space identifies the possible IT Services that an IT Service Provider may wish to consider delivering.
Maturity	(Continual Service Improvement) A measure of the Reliability, Efficiency and Effectiveness of a Process, Function, Organization etc. The most mature Processes and Functions are formally aligned to Business Objectives and Strategy, and are supported by a framework for continual improvement.
Maturity Level	A named level in a Maturity model such as the Carnegie Mellon Capability Maturity Model Integration.
Mean Time Between Failures (MTBF)	(Service Design) A Metric for measuring and reporting Reliability. MTBF is the average time that a Configuration Item or IT Service can perform its agreed Function without interruption. This is measured from when the CI or IT Service starts working, until it next fails.
Mean Time Between Service Incidents (MTBSI)	(Service Design) A Metric used for measuring and reporting Reliability. MTBSI is the mean time from when a System or IT Service fails, until it next fails. MTBSI is equal to MTBF + MTRS.
Mean Time To Repair (MTTR)	The average time taken to repair a Configuration Item or IT Service after a Failure. MTTR is measured from when the CI or IT Service fails until it is Repaired. MTTR does not include the time required to Recover or Restore. MTTR is sometimes incorrectly used to mean Mean Time to Restore Service.
Mean Time to Restore Service (MTRS)	The average time taken to Restore a Configuration Item or IT Service after a Failure. MTRS is measured from when the CI or IT Service fails until it is fully Restored and delivering its normal functionality. See Maintainability, Mean Time to Repair.
Metric	(Continual Service Improvement) Something that is measured and reported to help manage a Process, IT Service or Activity. See KPI.
Middleware	(Service Design) Software that connects two or more software Components or Applications. Middleware is usually purchased from a Supplier, rather than developed within the IT Service Provider. See Off the Shelf.
Mission Statement	The Mission Statement of an Organization is a short but complete description of the overall purpose and intentions of that Organization. It states what is to be achieved, but not how this should be done.
Model	A representation of a System, Process, IT Service, Configuration Item etc. that is used to help understand or predict future behavior.

Modeling	A technique that is used to predict the future behavior of a System, Process, IT Service, Configuration Item etc. Modeling is commonly used in Financial Management, Capacity Management and Availability Management.
Monitor Control Loop	(Service Operation) Monitoring the output of a Task, Process, IT Service or Configuration Item; comparing this output to a predefined norm; and taking appropriate action based on this comparison.
Monitoring	(Service Operation) Repeated observation of a Configuration Item, IT Service or Process to detect Events and to ensure that the current status is known.
Near-Shore	(Service Strategy) Provision of Services from a country near the country where the Customer is based. This can be the provision of an IT Service, or of supporting Functions such as Service Desk. See On-shore, Off-shore.
Net Present Value (NPV)	(Service Strategy) A technique used to help make decisions about Capital Expenditure. NPV compares cash inflows to cash outflows. Positive NPV indicates that an investment is worthwhile. See Internal Rate of Return, Return on Investment.
Notional Charging	(Service Strategy) An approach to Charging for IT Services. Charges to Customers are calculated and Customers are informed of the charge, but no money is actually transferred. Notional Charging is sometimes introduced to ensure that Customers are aware of the Costs they incur, or as a stage during the introduction of real Charging.
Objective	The defined purpose or aim of a Process, an Activity or an Organization as a whole. Objectives are usually expressed as measurable targets. The term Objective is also informally used to mean a Requirement. See Outcome.
Off the Shelf	Synonym for Commercial Off the Shelf.
Office of Government Commerce (OGC)	OGC owns the ITIL brand (copyright and trademark). OGC is a UK Government department that supports the delivery of the government's procurement agenda through its work in collaborative procurement and in raising levels of procurement skills and capability with departments. It also provides support for complex public sector projects.
Office of Public Sector Information (OPSI)	OPSI license the Crown Copyright material used in the ITIL publications. They are a UK Government department who provide online access to UK legislation, license the re-use of Crown copyright material, manage the Information Fair Trader Scheme, maintain the Government's Information Asset Register and provide advice and guidance on official publishing and Crown copyright.
Off-shore	(Service Strategy) Provision of Services from a location outside the country where the Customer is based, often in a different continent. This can be the provision of an IT Service, or of supporting Functions such as Service Desk. See On-shore, Near-shore.

On-shore	(Service Strategy) Provision of Services from a location within the country where the Customer is based. See Off-shore, Near-shore.
Operate	To perform as expected. A Process or Configuration Item is said to Operate if it is delivering the Required outputs. Operate also means to perform one or more Operations. For example, to Operate a computer is to do the day-to-day Operations needed for it to perform as expected.
Operation	(Service Operation) Day-to-day management of an IT Service, System, or other Configuration Item. Operation is also used to mean any pre-defined Activity or Transaction. For example loading a magnetic tape, accepting money at a point of sale, or reading data from a disk drive.
Operational	The lowest of three levels of Planning and delivery (Strategic, Tactical, Operational). Operational Activities include the day-to-day or short term Planning or delivery of a Business Process or IT Service Management Process. The term Operational is also a synonym for Live.
Operational Cost	Cost resulting from running the IT Services. Often repeating payments. For example staff costs, hardware maintenance and electricity (also known as "current expenditure" or "revenue expenditure"). See Capital Expenditure.
Operational Expenditure (OPEX)	Synonym for Operational Cost.
Operational Level Agreement (OLA)	(Service Design) (Continual Service Improvement) An Agreement between an IT Service Provider and another part of the same Organization. An OLA supports the IT Service Provider's delivery of IT Services to Customers. The OLA defines the goods or Services to be provided and the responsibilities of both parties. For example there could be an OLA • between the IT Service Provider and a procurement department to obtain hardware in agreed times • between the Service Desk and a Support Group to provide Incident Resolution in agreed times. See Service Level Agreement.
Operations Bridge	(Service Operation) A physical location where IT Services and IT Infrastructure are monitored and managed.
Operations Control	Synonym for IT Operations Control.
Operations Management	Synonym for IT Operations Management.
Opportunity Cost	(Service Strategy) A Cost that is used in deciding between investment choices. Opportunity Cost represents the revenue that would have been generated by using the Resources in a different way. For example the Opportunity Cost of purchasing a new Server may include not carrying out a Service Improvement activity that the money could have been spent on. Opportunity cost analysis is used as part of a decision making processes, but is not treated as an actual Cost in any financial statement.

Optimize	Review, Plan and request Changes, in order to obtain the maximum Efficiency and Effectiveness from a Process, Configuration Item, Application etc.
Organization	A company, legal entity or other institution. Examples of Organizations that are not companies include International Standards Organization or itSMF. The term Organization is sometimes used to refer to any entity which has People, Resources and Budgets. For example a Project or Business Unit.
Outcome	The result of carrying out an Activity; following a Process; delivering an IT Service etc. The term Outcome is used to refer to intended results, as well as to actual results. See Objective.
Outsourcing	(Service Strategy) Using an External Service Provider to manage IT Services. See Service Sourcing, Type III Service Provider.
Overhead	Synonym for Indirect cost
Pain Value Analysis	(Service Operation) A technique used to help identify the Business Impact of one or more Problems. A formula is used to calculate Pain Value based on the number of Users affected, the duration of the Downtime, the Impact on each User, and the cost to the Business (if known).
Pareto Principle	(Service Operation) A technique used to priorities Activities. The Pareto Principle says that 80% of the value of any Activity is created with 20% of the effort. Pareto Analysis is also used in Problem Management to priorities possible Problem causes for investigation.
Partnership	A relationship between two Organizations which involves working closely together for common goals or mutual benefit. The IT Service Provider should have a Partnership with the Business, and with Third Parties who are critical to the delivery of IT Services. See Value Network.
Passive Monitoring	(Service Operation) Monitoring of a Configuration Item, an IT Service or a Process that relies on an Alert or notification to discover the current status. See Active Monitoring.
Pattern of Business Activity (PBA)	(Service Strategy) A Workload profile of one or more Business Activities. Patterns of Business Activity are used to help the IT Service Provider understand and plan for different levels of Business Activity. See User Profile.
Percentage utilization	(Service Design) The amount of time that a Component is busy over a given period of time. For example, if a CPU is busy for 1800 seconds in a one hour period, its utilization is 50%
Performance	A measure of what is achieved or delivered by a System, person, team, Process, or IT Service.

Performance Anatomy	(Service Strategy) An approach to Organizational Culture that integrates, and actively manages, leadership and strategy, people development, technology enablement, performance management and innovation.
Performance Management	(Continual Service Improvement) The Process responsible for day-to-day Capacity Management Activities. These include Monitoring, Threshold detection, Performance analysis and Tuning, and implementing Changes related to Performance and Capacity.
Pilot	(Service Transition) A limited Deployment of an IT Service, a Release or a Process to the Live Environment. A Pilot is used to reduce Risk and to gain User feedback and Acceptance. See Test, Evaluation.
Plan	A detailed proposal which describes the Activities and Resources needed to achieve an Objective. For example a Plan to implement a new IT Service or Process. ISO/IEC 20000 requires a Plan for the management of each IT Service Management Process.
Plan-Do-Check-Act	(Continual Service Improvement) A four stage cycle for Process management, attributed to Edward Deming. Plan-Do-Check-Act is also called the Deming Cycle. PLAN: Design or revise Processes that support the IT Services. DO: Implement the Plan and manage the Processes. CHECK: Measure the Processes and IT Services, compare with Objectives and produce reports ACT: Plan and implement Changes to improve the Processes.
Planned Downtime	(Service Design) Agreed time when an IT Service will not be available. Planned Downtime is often used for maintenance, upgrades and testing. See Change Window, Downtime.
Planning	An Activity responsible for creating one or more Plans. For example, Capacity Planning.
PMBOK	A Project management Standard maintained and published by the Project Management Institute. PMBOK stands for Project Management Body of Knowledge. See http://www.pmi.org/ for more information. See PRINCE2.
Policy	Formally documented management expectations and intentions. Policies are used to direct decisions, and to ensure consistent and appropriate development and implementation of Processes, Standards, Roles, Activities, IT Infrastructure etc.
Portable Facility	(Service Design) A prefabricated building, or a large vehicle, provided by a Third Party and moved to a site when needed by an IT Service Continuity Plan. See Recovery Option, Fixed Facility.
Post Implementation Review (PIR)	A Review that takes place after a Change or a Project has been implemented. A PIR determines if the Change or Project was successful, and identifies opportunities for improvement.

Practice	A way of working, or a way in which work must be done. Practices can include Activities, Processes, Functions, Standards and Guidelines. See Best Practice.
Prerequisite for Success (PFS)	An Activity that needs to be completed, or a condition that needs to be met, to enable successful implementation of a Plan or Process. A PFS is often an output from one Process that is a required input to another Process.
Pricing	(Service Strategy) The Activity for establishing how much Customers will be Charged.
PRINCE2	The standard UK government methodology for Project management. See http://www.ogc.gov.uk/prince2/ for more information. See PMBOK.
Priority	(Service Transition) (Service Operation) A Category used to identify the relative importance of an Incident, Problem or Change. Priority is based on Impact and Urgency, and is used to identify required times for actions to be taken. For example the SLA may state that Priority2 Incidents must be resolved within 12 hours.
Proactive Monitoring	(Service Operation) Monitoring that looks for patterns of Events to predict possible future Failures. See Reactive Monitoring.
Proactive Problem Management	(Service Operation) Part of the Problem Management Process. The Objective of Proactive Problem Management is to identify Problems that might otherwise be missed. Proactive Problem Management analyses Incident Records, and uses data collected by other IT Service Management Processes to identify trends or significant Problems.
Problem	(Service Operation) A cause of one or more Incidents. The cause is not usually known at the time a Problem Record is created, and the Problem Management Process is responsible for further investigation.
Problem Management	(Service Operation) The Process responsible for managing the Lifecycle of all Problems. The primary Objectives of Problem Management are to prevent Incidents from happening, and to minimize the Impact of Incidents that cannot be prevented.
Problem Record	(Service Operation) A Record containing the details of a Problem. Each Problem Record documents the Lifecycle of a single Problem.
Procedure	A Document containing steps that specify how to achieve an Activity. Procedures are defined as part of Processes. See Work Instruction.
Process	A structured set of Activities designed to accomplish a specific Objective. A Process takes one or more defined inputs and turns them into defined outputs. A Process may include any of the Roles, responsibilities, tools and management Controls required to reliably deliver the outputs. A Process may define Policies, Standards, Guidelines, Activities, and Work Instructions if they are needed.

Process Control   The Activity of planning and regulating a Process, with the Objective of performing the Process in an Effective, Efficient, and consistent manner.

Process Manager   A Role responsible for Operational management of a Process. The Process Manager's responsibilities include Planning and coordination of all Activities required to carry out, monitor and report on the Process. There may be several Process Managers for one Process, for example regional Change Managers or IT Service Continuity Managers for each data centre. The Process Manager Role is often assigned to the person who carries out the Process Owner Role, but the two Roles may be separate in larger Organizations.

Process Owner   A Role responsible for ensuring that a Process is Fit for Purpose. The Process Owner's responsibilities include sponsorship, Design, Change Management and continual improvement of the Process and its Metrics. This Role is often assigned to the same person who carries out the Process Manager Role, but the two Roles may be separate in larger Organizations.

Production Environment   Synonym for Live Environment.

Profit Centre   (Service Strategy) A Business Unit which charges for Services provided. A Profit Centre can be created with the objective of making a profit, recovering Costs, or running at a loss. An IT Service Provider can be run as a Cost Centre or a Profit Centre.

pro-forma   A template, or example Document containing example data that will be replaced with the real values when these are available.

Program   A number of Projects and Activities that are planned and managed together to achieve an overall set of related Objectives and other Outcomes.

Project   A temporary Organization, with people and other Assets required to achieve an Objective or other Outcome. Each Project has a Lifecycle that typically includes initiation, Planning, execution, Closure etc. Projects are usually managed using a formal methodology such as PRINCE2.

Projected Service Outage (PSO)   (Service Transition) A Document that identifies the effect of planned Changes, maintenance Activities and Test Plans on agreed Service Levels.

PRojects IN Controlled Environments (PRINCE2)   See PRINCE2

Qualification   (Service Transition) An Activity that ensures that IT Infrastructure is appropriate, and correctly configured, to support an Application or IT Service.
See Validation.

Quality	The ability of a product, Service, or Process to provide the intended value. For example, a hardware Component can be considered to be of high Quality if it performs as expected and delivers the required Reliability. Process Quality also requires an ability to monitor Effectiveness and Efficiency, and to improve them if necessary. See Quality Management System.
Quality Assurance (QA)	(Service Transition) The Process responsible for ensuring that the Quality of a product, Service or Process will provide its intended Value.
Quality Management System (QMS)	(Continual Service Improvement) The set of Processes responsible for ensuring that all work carried out by an Organization is of a suitable Quality to reliably meet Business Objectives or Service Levels. See ISO 9000.
Quick Win	(Continual Service Improvement) An improvement Activity which is expected to provide a Return on Investment in a short period of time with relatively small Cost and effort. See Pareto Principle.
RACI	(Service Design) (Continual Service Improvement) A Model used to help define Roles and Responsibilities. RACI stands for Responsible, Accountable, Consulted and Informed. See Stakeholder.
Reactive Monitoring	(Service Operation) Monitoring that takes action in response to an Event. For example submitting a batch job when the previous job completes, or logging an Incident when an Error occurs. See Proactive Monitoring.
Reciprocal Arrangement	(Service Design) A Recovery Option. An agreement between two Organizations to share resources in an emergency. For example, Computer Room space or use of a mainframe.
Record	A Document containing the results or other output from a Process or Activity. Records are evidence of the fact that an Activity took place and may be paper or electronic. For example, an Audit report, an Incident Record, or the minutes of a meeting.
Recovery	(Service Design) (Service Operation) Returning a Configuration Item or an IT Service to a working state. Recovery of an IT Service often includes recovering data to a known consistent state. After Recovery, further steps may be needed before the IT Service can be made available to the Users (Restoration).
Recovery Option	(Service Design) A Strategy for responding to an interruption to Service. Commonly used Strategies are Do Nothing, Manual Workaround, Reciprocal Arrangement, Gradual Recovery, Intermediate Recovery, Fast Recovery, Immediate Recovery. Recovery Options may make use of dedicated facilities, or Third Party facilities shared by multiple Businesses.

Recovery Point Objective (RPO)	(Service Operation) The maximum amount of data that may be lost when Service is Restored after an interruption. Recovery Point Objective is expressed as a length of time before the Failure. For example a Recovery Point Objective of one day may be supported by daily Backups, and up to 24 hours of data may be lost. Recovery Point Objectives for each IT Service should be negotiated, agreed and documented, and used as Requirements for Service Design and IT Service Continuity Plans.
Recovery Time Objective (RTO)	(Service Operation) The maximum time allowed for recovery of an IT Service following an interruption. The Service Level to be provided may be less than normal Service Level Targets. Recovery Time Objectives for each IT Service should be negotiated, agreed and documented. See Business Impact Analysis.
Redundancy	Synonym for Fault Tolerance. The term Redundant also has a generic meaning of obsolete, or no longer needed.
Relationship	A connection or interaction between two people or things. In Business Relationship Management it is the interaction between the IT Service Provider and the Business. In Configuration Management it is a link between two Configuration Items that identifies a dependency or connection between them. For example Applications may be linked to the Servers they run on, IT Services have many links to all the CIs that contribute to them.
Relationship Processes	The ISO/IEC 20000 Process group that includes Business Relationship Management and Supplier Management.
Release	(Service Transition) A collection of hardware, software, documentation, Processes or other Components required to implement one or more approved Changes to IT Services. The contents of each Release are managed, Tested, and Deployed as a single entity.
Release and Deployment Management	(Service Transition) The Process responsible for both Release Management and Deployment.
Release Identification	(Service Transition) A naming convention used to uniquely identify a Release. The Release Identification typically includes a reference to the Configuration Item and a version number. For example Microsoft Office 2003 SR2.
Release Management	(Service Transition) The Process responsible for Planning, scheduling and controlling the movement of Releases to Test and Live Environments. The primary Objective of Release Management is to ensure that the integrity of the Live Environment is protected and that the correct Components are released. Release Management is part of the Release and Deployment Management Process.
Release Process	The name used by ISO/IEC 20000 for the Process group that includes Release Management. This group does not include any other Processes. Release Process is also used as a synonym for Release Management Process.

Release Record	(Service Transition) A Record in the CMDB that defines the content of a Release. A Release Record has Relationships with all Configuration Items that are affected by the Release.
Release Unit	(Service Transition) Components of an IT Service that are normally Released together. A Release Unit typically includes sufficient Components to perform a useful Function. For example one Release Unit could be a Desktop PC, including Hardware, Software, Licenses, Documentation etc. A different Release Unit may be the complete Payroll Application, including IT Operations Procedures and User training.
Release Window	Synonym for Change Window.
Reliability	(Service Design) (Continual Service Improvement) A measure of how long a Configuration Item or IT Service can perform its agreed Function without interruption. Usually measured as MTBF or MTBSI. The term Reliability can also be used to state how likely it is that a Process, Function etc. will deliver its required outputs. See Availability.
Remediation	(Service Transition) Recovery to a known state after a failed Change or Release.
Repair	(Service Operation) The replacement or correction of a failed Configuration Item.
Request for Change (RFC)	(Service Transition) A formal proposal for a Change to be made. An RFC includes details of the proposed Change, and may be recorded on paper or electronically. The term RFC is often misused to mean a Change Record, or the Change itself.
Request Fulfilment	(Service Operation) The Process responsible for managing the Lifecycle of all Service Requests.
Requirement	(Service Design) A formal statement of what is needed. For example a Service Level Requirement, a Project Requirement or the required Deliverables for a Process. See Statement of Requirements.
Resilience	(Service Design) The ability of a Configuration Item or IT Service to resist Failure or to Recover quickly following a Failure. For example, an armored cable will resist failure when put under stress. See Fault Tolerance.
Resolution	(Service Operation) Action taken to repair the Root Cause of an Incident or Problem, or to implement a Workaround. In ISO/IEC 20000, Resolution Processes is the Process group that includes Incident and Problem Management.
Resolution Processes	The ISO/IEC 20000 Process group that includes Incident Management and Problem Management.
Resource	(Service Strategy) A generic term that includes IT Infrastructure, people, money or anything else that might help to deliver an IT Service. Resources are considered to be Assets of an Organization. See Capability, Service Asset.

Response Time	A measure of the time taken to complete an Operation or Transaction. Used in Capacity Management as a measure of IT Infrastructure Performance, and in Incident Management as a measure of the time taken to answer the phone, or to start Diagnosis.
Responsiveness	A measurement of the time taken to respond to something. This could be Response Time of a Transaction, or the speed with which an IT Service Provider responds to an Incident or Request for Change etc.
Restoration of Service	See Restore.
Restore	(Service Operation) Taking action to return an IT Service to the Users after Repair and Recovery from an Incident. This is the primary Objective of Incident Management.
Retire	(Service Transition) Permanent removal of an IT Service, or other Configuration Item, from the Live Environment. Retired is a stage in the Lifecycle of many Configuration Items.
Return on Investment (ROI)	(Service Strategy) (Continual Service Improvement) A measurement of the expected benefit of an investment. In the simplest sense it is the net profit of an investment divided by the net worth of the assets invested. See Net Present Value, Value on Investment.
Return to Normal	(Service Design) The phase of an IT Service Continuity Plan during which full normal operations are resumed. For example, if an alternate data centre has been in use, then this phase will bring the primary data centre back into operation, and restore the ability to invoke IT Service Continuity Plans again.
Review	An evaluation of a Change, Problem, Process, Project etc. Reviews are typically carried out at predefined points in the Lifecycle, and especially after Closure. The purpose of a Review is to ensure that all Deliverables have been provided, and to identify opportunities for improvement. See Post Implementation Review.
Rights	(Service Operation) Entitlements, or permissions, granted to a User or Role. For example the Right to modify particular data, or to authorize a Change.
Risk	A possible Event that could cause harm or loss, or affect the ability to achieve Objectives. A Risk is measured by the probability of a Threat, the Vulnerability of the Asset to that Threat, and the Impact it would have if it occurred.
Risk Assessment	The initial steps of Risk Management. Analyzing the value of Assets to the business, identifying Threats to those Assets, and evaluating how Vulnerable each Asset is to those Threats. Risk Assessment can be quantitative (based on numerical data) or qualitative.
Risk Management	The Process responsible for identifying, assessing and controlling Risks. See Risk Assessment.

Role	A set of responsibilities, Activities and authorities granted to a person or team. A Role is defined in a Process. One person or team may have multiple Roles, for example the Roles of Configuration Manager and Change Manager may be carried out by a single person.
Rollout	(Service Transition) Synonym for Deployment. Most often used to refer to complex or phased Deployments or Deployments to multiple locations.
Root Cause	(Service Operation) The underlying or original cause of an Incident or Problem.
Root Cause Analysis (RCA)	(Service Operation) An Activity that identifies the Root Cause of an Incident or Problem. RCA typically concentrates on IT Infrastructure failures. See Service Failure Analysis.
Running Costs	Synonym for Operational Costs
Scalability	The ability of an IT Service, Process, Configuration Item etc. to perform its agreed Function when the Workload or Scope changes.
Scope	The boundary, or extent, to which a Process, Procedure, Certification, Contract etc. applies. For example the Scope of Change Management may include all Live IT Services and related Configuration Items, the Scope of an ISO/IEC 20000 Certificate may include all IT Services delivered out of a named data centre.
Second-line Support	(Service Operation) The second level in a hierarchy of Support Groups involved in the resolution of Incidents and investigation of Problems. Each level contains more specialist skills, or has more time or other Resources.
Security	See Information Security Management
Security Management	Synonym for Information Security Management
Security Policy	Synonym for Information Security Policy
Separation of Concerns (SoC)	(Service Strategy) An approach to Designing a solution or IT Service that divides the problem into pieces that can be solved independently. This approach separates "what" is to be done from "how" it is to be done.
Server	(Service Operation) A computer that is connected to a network and provides software Functions that are used by other computers.
Service	A means of delivering value to Customers by facilitating Outcomes Customers want to achieve without the ownership of specific Costs and Risks.
Service Acceptance Criteria (SAC)	(Service Transition) A set of criteria used to ensure that an IT Service meets its functionality and Quality Requirements and that the IT Service Provider is ready to Operate the new IT Service when it has been Deployed. See Acceptance.
Service Analytics	(Service Strategy) A technique used in the Assessment of the Business Impact of Incidents. Service Analytics Models the dependencies between Configuration Items, and the dependencies of IT Services on Configuration Items.

Service Asset	Any Capability or Resource of a Service Provider. See Asset.
Service Asset and Configuration Management (SACM)	(Service Transition) The Process responsible for both Configuration Management and Asset Management.
Service Capacity Management (SCM)	(Service Design) (Continual Service Improvement) The Activity responsible for understanding the Performance and Capacity of IT Services. The Resources used by each IT Service and the pattern of usage over time are collected, recorded, and analyzed for use in the Capacity Plan. See Business Capacity Management, Component Capacity Management.
Service Catalogue	(Service Design) A database or structured Document with information about all Live IT Services, including those available for Deployment. The Service Catalogue is the only part of the Service Portfolio published to Customers, and is used to support the sale and delivery of IT Services. The Service Catalogue includes information about deliverables, prices, contact points, ordering and request Processes. See Contract Portfolio.
Service Continuity Management	Synonym for IT Service Continuity Management.
Service Contract	(Service Strategy) A Contract to deliver one or more IT Services. The term Service Contract is also used to mean any Agreement to deliver IT Services, whether this is a legal Contract or an SLA. See Contract Portfolio.
Service Culture	A Customer oriented Culture. The major Objectives of a Service Culture are Customer satisfaction and helping the Customer to achieve their Business Objectives.
Service Design	(Service Design) A stage in the Lifecycle of an IT Service. Service Design includes a number of Processes and Functions and is the title of one of the Core ITIL publications. See Design.
Service Design Package	(Service Design) Document(s) defining all aspects of an IT Service and its Requirements through each stage of its Lifecycle. A Service Design Package is produced for each new IT Service, major Change, or IT Service Retirement.
Service Desk	(Service Operation) The Single Point of Contact between the Service Provider and the Users. A typical Service Desk manages Incidents and Service Requests, and also handles communication with the Users.
Service Failure Analysis (SFA)	(Service Design) An Activity that identifies underlying causes of one or more IT Service interruptions. SFA identifies opportunities to improve the IT Service Provider's Processes and tools, and not just the IT Infrastructure. SFA is a time constrained, project-like activity, rather than an ongoing process of analysis. See Root Cause Analysis.

Service Hours	(Service Design) (Continual Service Improvement) An agreed time period when a particular IT Service should be Available. For example, "Monday-Friday 08:00 to 17:00 except public holidays". Service Hours should be defined in a Service Level Agreement.
Service Improvement Plan (SIP)	(Continual Service Improvement) A formal Plan to implement improvements to a Process or IT Service.
Service Knowledge Management System (SKMS)	(Service Transition) A set of tools and databases that are used to manage knowledge and information. The SKMS includes the Configuration Management System, as well as other tools and databases. The SKMS stores, manages, updates, and presents all information that an IT Service Provider needs to manage the full Lifecycle of IT Services.
Service Level	Measured and reported achievement against one or more Service Level Targets. The term Service Level is sometimes used informally to mean Service Level Target.
Service Level Agreement (SLA)	(Service Design) (Continual Service Improvement) An Agreement between an IT Service Provider and a Customer. The SLA describes the IT Service, documents Service Level Targets, and specifies the responsibilities of the IT Service Provider and the Customer. A single SLA may cover multiple IT Services or multiple Customers. See Operational Level Agreement.
Service Level Management (SLM)	(Service Design) (Continual Service Improvement) The Process responsible for negotiating Service Level Agreements, and ensuring that these are met. SLM is responsible for ensuring that all IT Service Management Processes, Operational Level Agreements, and Underpinning Contracts, are appropriate for the agreed Service Level Targets. SLM monitors and reports on Service Levels, and holds regular Customer reviews.
Service Level Package (SLP)	(Service Strategy) A defined level of Utility and Warranty for a particular Service Package. Each SLP is designed to meet the needs of a particular Pattern of Business Activity. See Line of Service.
Service Level Requirement (SLR)	(Service Design) (Continual Service Improvement) A Customer Requirement for an aspect of an IT Service. SLRs are based on Business Objectives and are used to negotiate agreed Service Level Targets.
Service Level Target	(Service Design) (Continual Service Improvement) A commitment that is documented in a Service Level Agreement. Service Level Targets are based on Service Level Requirements, and are needed to ensure that the IT Service design is Fit for Purpose. Service Level Targets should be SMART, and are usually based on KPIs.
Service Maintenance Objective	(Service Operation) The expected time that a Configuration Item will be unavailable due to planned maintenance Activity.
Service Management	Service Management is a set of specialized organizational capabilities for providing value to customers in the form of services.

Service Management Lifecycle	An approach to IT Service Management that emphasizes the importance of coordination and Control across the various Functions, Processes, and Systems necessary to manage the full Lifecycle of IT Services. The Service Management Lifecycle approach considers the Strategy, Design, Transition, Operation and Continuous Improvement of IT Services.
Service Manager	A manager who is responsible for managing the end-to-end Lifecycle of one or more IT Services. The term Service Manager is also used to mean any manager within the IT Service Provider. Most commonly used to refer to a Business Relationship Manager, a Process Manager, an Account Manager or a senior manager with responsibility for IT Services overall.
Service Operation	(Service Operation) A stage in the Lifecycle of an IT Service. Service Operation includes a number of Processes and Functions and is the title of one of the Core ITIL publications. See Operation.
Service Owner	(Continual Service Improvement) A Role which is accountable for the delivery of a specific IT Service.
Service Package	(Service Strategy) A detailed description of an IT Service that is available to be delivered to Customers. A Service Package includes a Service Level Package and one or more Core Services and Supporting Services.
Service Pipeline	(Service Strategy) A database or structured Document listing all IT Services that are under consideration or Development, but are not yet available to Customers. The Service Pipeline provides a Business view of possible future IT Services and is part of the Service Portfolio which is not normally published to Customers.
Service Portfolio	(Service Strategy) The complete set of Services that are managed by a Service Provider. The Service Portfolio is used to manage the entire Lifecycle of all Services, and includes three Categories: Service Pipeline (proposed or in Development); Service Catalogue (Live or available for Deployment); and Retired Services. See Service Portfolio Management, Contract Portfolio.
Service Portfolio Management (SPM)	(Service Strategy) The Process responsible for managing the Service Portfolio. Service Portfolio Management considers Services in terms of the Business value that they provide.
Service Potential	(Service Strategy) The total possible value of the overall Capabilities and Resources of the IT Service Provider.
Service Provider	(Service Strategy) An Organization supplying Services to one or more Internal Customers or External Customers. Service Provider is often used as an abbreviation for IT Service Provider. See Type I Service Provider, Type II Service Provider, Type III Service Provider.
Service Provider Interface (SPI)	(Service Strategy) An interface between the IT Service Provider and a User, Customer, Business Process, or a Supplier. Analysis of Service Provider Interfaces helps to coordinate end-to-end management of IT Services.

Service Provisioning Optimization (SPO)	(Service Strategy) Analyzing the finances and constraints of an IT Service to decide if alternative approaches to Service delivery might reduce Costs or improve Quality.
Service Reporting	(Continual Service Improvement) The Process responsible for producing and delivering reports of achievement and trends against Service Levels. Service Reporting should agree the format, content and frequency of reports with Customers.
Service Request	(Service Operation) A request from a User for information, or advice, or for a Standard Change or for Access to an IT Service. For example to reset a password, or to provide standard IT Services for a new User. Service Requests are usually handled by a Service Desk, and do not require an RFC to be submitted. See Request Fulfilment.
Service Sourcing	(Service Strategy) The Strategy and approach for deciding whether to provide a Service internally or to Outsource it to an External Service Provider. Service Sourcing also means the execution of this Strategy. Service Sourcing includes:

- Internal Sourcing - Internal or Shared Services using Type I or Type II Service Providers.
- Traditional Sourcing - Full Service Outsourcing using a Type III Service Provider.
- Multivendor Sourcing - Prime, Consortium or Selective Outsourcing using Type III Service Providers.

Service Strategy	(Service Strategy) The title of one of the Core ITIL publications. Service Strategy establishes an overall Strategy for IT Services and for IT Service Management.
Service Transition	(Service Transition) A stage in the Lifecycle of an IT Service. Service Transition includes a number of Processes and Functions and is the title of one of the Core ITIL publications. See Transition.
Service Utility	(Service Strategy) The Functionality of an IT Service from the Customer's perspective. The Business value of an IT Service is created by the combination of Service Utility (what the Service does) and Service Warranty (how well it does it). See Utility.
Service Validation and Testing	(Service Transition) The Process responsible for Validation and Testing of a new or Changed IT Service. Service Validation and Testing ensures that the IT Service matches its Design Specification and will meet the needs of the Business.
Service Valuation	(Service Strategy) A measurement of the total Cost of delivering an IT Service, and the total value to the Business of that IT Service. Service Valuation is used to help the Business and the IT Service Provider agree on the value of the IT Service.
Service Warranty	(Service Strategy) Assurance that an IT Service will meet agreed Requirements. This may be a formal Agreement such as a Service Level Agreement or Contract, or may be a marketing message or brand image. The Business value of an IT Service is created by the combination of Service Utility (what the Service does) and Service Warranty (how well it does it). See Warranty.

Serviceability	(Service Design) (Continual Service Improvement) The ability of a Third Party Supplier to meet the terms of their Contract. This Contract will include agreed levels of Reliability, Maintainability or Availability for a Configuration Item.
Shift	(Service Operation) A group or team of people who carry out a specific Role for a fixed period of time. For example there could be four shifts of IT Operations Control personnel to support an IT Service that is used 24 hours a day.
Simulation modeling	(Service Design) (Continual Service Improvement) A technique that creates a detailed Model to predict the behavior of a Configuration Item or IT Service. Simulation Models can be very accurate but are expensive and time consuming to create. A Simulation Model is often created by using the actual Configuration Items that are being modeled, with artificial Workloads or Transactions. They are used in Capacity Management when accurate results are important. A simulation model is sometimes called a Performance Benchmark.
Single Point of Contact	(Service Operation) Providing a single consistent way to communicate with an Organization or Business Unit. For example, a Single Point of Contact for an IT Service Provider is usually called a Service Desk.
Single Point of Failure (SPOF)	(Service Design) Any Configuration Item that can cause an Incident when it fails, and for which a Countermeasure has not been implemented. A SPOF may be a person, or a step in a Process or Activity, as well as a Component of the IT Infrastructure. See Failure.
SLAM Chart	(Continual Service Improvement) A Service Level Agreement Monitoring Chart is used to help monitor and report achievements against Service Level Targets. A SLAM Chart is typically color coded to show whether each agreed Service Level Target has been met, missed, or nearly missed during each of the previous 12 months.
SMART	(Service Design) (Continual Service Improvement) An acronym for helping to remember that targets in Service Level Agreements and Project Plans should be Specific, Measurable, Achievable, Relevant and Timely.
Snapshot	(Service Transition) The current state of a Configuration as captured by a discovery tool. Also used as a synonym for Benchmark. See Baseline.
Source	See Service Sourcing.
Specification	A formal definition of Requirements. A Specification may be used to define technical or Operational Requirements, and may be internal or external. Many public Standards consist of a Code of Practice and a Specification. The Specification defines the Standard against which an Organization can be Audited.

Stakeholder	All people who have an interest in an Organization, Project, IT Service etc. Stakeholders may be interested in the Activities, targets, Resources, or Deliverables. Stakeholders may include Customers, Partners, employees, shareholders, owners, etc. See RACI.
Standard	A mandatory Requirement. Examples include ISO/IEC 20000 (an international Standard), an internal security Standard for Unix configuration, or a government Standard for how financial Records should be maintained. The term Standard is also used to refer to a Code of Practice or Specification published by a Standards Organization such as ISO or BSI. See Guideline.
Standard Change	(Service Transition) A pre-approved Change that is low Risk, relatively common and follows a Procedure or Work Instruction. For example password reset or provision of standard equipment to a new employee. RFCs are not required to implement a Standard Change, and they are logged and tracked using a different mechanism, such as a Service Request. See Change Model.
Standard Operating Procedures (SOP)	(Service Operation) Procedures used by IT Operations Management.
Standby	(Service Design) Used to refer to Resources that are not required to deliver the Live IT Services, but are available to support IT Service Continuity Plans. For example a Standby data centre may be maintained to support Hot Standby, Warm Standby or Cold Standby arrangements.
Statement of requirements (SOR)	(Service Design) A Document containing all Requirements for a product purchase, or a new or changed IT Service. See Terms of Reference.
Status	The name of a required field in many types of Record. It shows the current stage in the Lifecycle of the associated Configuration Item, Incident, Problem etc.
Status Accounting	(Service Transition) The Activity responsible for recording and reporting the Lifecycle of each Configuration Item.
Storage Management	(Service Operation) The Process responsible for managing the storage and maintenance of data throughout its Lifecycle.
Strategic	(Service Strategy) The highest of three levels of Planning and delivery (Strategic, Tactical, Operational). Strategic Activities include Objective setting and long term Planning to achieve the overall Vision.
Strategy	(Service Strategy) A Strategic Plan designed to achieve defined Objectives.
Super User	(Service Operation) A User who helps other Users, and assists in communication with the Service Desk or other parts of the IT Service Provider. Super Users typically provide support for minor Incidents and training.

Supplier	(Service Strategy) (Service Design) A Third Party responsible for supplying goods or Services that are required to deliver IT services. Examples of suppliers include commodity hardware and software vendors, network and telecom providers, and Outsourcing Organizations. See Underpinning Contract, Supply Chain.
Supplier and Contract Database (SCD)	(Service Design) A database or structured Document used to manage Supplier Contracts throughout their Lifecycle. The SCD contains key Attributes of all Contracts with Suppliers, and should be part of the Service Knowledge Management System.
Supplier Management	(Service Design) The Process responsible for ensuring that all Contracts with Suppliers support the needs of the Business, and that all Suppliers meet their contractual commitments.
Supply Chain	(Service Strategy) The Activities in a Value Chain carried out by Suppliers. A Supply Chain typically involves multiple Suppliers, each adding value to the product or Service. See Value Network.
Support Group	(Service Operation) A group of people with technical skills. Support Groups provide the Technical Support needed by all of the IT Service Management Processes. See Technical Management.
Support Hours	(Service Design) (Service Operation) The times or hours when support is available to the Users. Typically this is the hours when the Service Desk is available. Support Hours should be defined in a Service Level Agreement, and may be different from Service Hours. For example, Service Hours may be 24 hours a day, but the Support Hours may be 07:00 to 19:00.
Supporting Service	(Service Strategy) A Service that enables or enhances a Core Service. For example a Directory Service or a Backup Service. See Service Package.
SWOT Analysis	(Continual Service Improvement) A technique that reviews and analyses the internal strengths and weaknesses of an Organization and the external opportunities and threats which it faces SWOT stands for Strengths, Weaknesses, Opportunities and Threats.
System	A number of related things that work together to achieve an overall Objective. For example: • A computer System including hardware, software and Applications. • A management System, including multiple Processes that are planned and managed together. For example a Quality Management System. • A Database Management System or Operating System that includes many software modules that are designed to perform a set of related Functions.
System Management	The part of IT Service Management that focuses on the management of IT Infrastructure rather than Process.

Tactical	The middle of three levels of Planning and delivery (Strategic, Tactical, Operational). Tactical Activities include the medium term Plans required to achieve specific Objectives, typically over a period of weeks to months.
Tag	(Service Strategy) A short code used to identify a Category. For example tags EC1, EC2, EC3 etc. might be used to identify different Customer outcomes when analyzing and comparing Strategies. The term Tag is also used to refer to the Activity of assigning Tags to things.
Technical Management	(Service Operation) The Function responsible for providing technical skills in support of IT Services and management of the IT Infrastructure. Technical Management defines the Roles of Support Groups, as well as the tools, Processes and Procedures required.
Technical Observation (TO)	(Continual Service Improvement) A technique used in Service Improvement, Problem investigation and Availability Management. Technical support staff meet to monitor the behavior and Performance of an IT Service and make recommendations for improvement.
Technical Service	Synonym for Infrastructure Service.
Technical Support	Synonym for Technical Management.
Tension Metrics	(Continual Service Improvement) A set of related Metrics, in which improvements to one Metric have a negative effect on another. Tension Metrics are designed to ensure that an appropriate balance is achieved.
Terms of Reference (TOR)	(Service Design) A Document specifying the Requirements, Scope, Deliverables, Resources and schedule for a Project or Activity.
Test	(Service Transition) An Activity that verifies that a Configuration Item, IT Service, Process, etc. meets its Specification or agreed Requirements. See Service Validation and Testing, Acceptance.
Test Environment	(Service Transition) A controlled Environment used to Test Configuration Items, Builds, IT Services, Processes etc.
Third Party	A person, group, or Business who is not part of the Service Level Agreement for an IT Service, but is required to ensure successful delivery of that IT Service. For example a software Supplier, a hardware maintenance company, or a facilities department. Requirements for Third Parties are typically specified in Underpinning Contracts or Operational Level Agreements.
Third-line Support	(Service Operation) The third level in a hierarchy of Support Groups involved in the resolution of Incidents and investigation of Problems. Each level contains more specialist skills, or has more time or other Resources.
Threat	Anything that might exploit a Vulnerability. Any potential cause of an Incident can be considered to be a Threat. For example a fire is a Threat that could exploit the Vulnerability of flammable floor coverings. This term is commonly used in Information Security Management and IT Service Continuity Management, but also applies to other areas such as Problem and Availability Management.

Threshold	The value of a Metric which should cause an Alert to be generated, or management action to be taken. For example "Priority1 Incident not solved within 4 hours", "more than 5 soft disk errors in an hour", or "more than 10 failed changes in a month".
Throughput	(Service Design) A measure of the number of Transactions, or other Operations, performed in a fixed time. For example 5000 emails sent per hour, or 200 disk I/Os per second.
Total Cost of Ownership (TCO)	(Service Strategy) A methodology used to help make investment decisions. TCO assesses the full Lifecycle Cost of owning a Configuration Item, not just the initial Cost or purchase price. See Total Cost of Utilization.
Total Cost of Utilization (TCU)	(Service Strategy) A methodology used to help make investment and Service Sourcing decisions. TCU assesses the full Lifecycle Cost to the Customer of using an IT Service. See Total Cost of Ownership.
Total Quality Management (TQM)	(Continual Service Improvement) A methodology for managing continual Improvement by using a Quality Management System. TQM establishes a Culture involving all people in the Organization in a Process of continual monitoring and improvement.
Transaction	A discrete Function performed by an IT Service. For example transferring money from one bank account to another. A single Transaction may involve numerous additions, deletions and modifications of data. Either all of these complete successfully or none of them is carried out.
Transition	(Service Transition) A change in state, corresponding to a movement of an IT Service or other Configuration Item from one Lifecycle status to the next.
Transition Planning and Support	(Service Transition) The Process responsible for Planning all Service Transition Processes and co-coordinating the resources that they require. These Service Transition Processes are Change Management, Service Asset and Configuration Management, Release and Deployment Management, Service Validation and Testing, Evaluation, and Knowledge Management.
Trend Analysis	(Continual Service Improvement) Analysis of data to identify time related patterns. Trend Analysis is used in Problem Management to identify common Failures or fragile Configuration Items, and in Capacity Management as a Modeling tool to predict future behavior. It is also used as a management tool for identifying deficiencies in IT Service Management Processes.
Tuning	The Activity responsible for Planning Changes to make the most efficient use of Resources. Tuning is part of Performance Management, which also includes Performance Monitoring and implementation of the required Changes.
Type I Service Provider	(Service Strategy) An Internal Service Provider that is embedded within a Business Unit. There may be several Type I Service Providers within an Organization.

Type II Service Provider	(Service Strategy) An Internal Service Provider that provides shared IT Services to more than one Business Unit.
Type III Service Provider	(Service Strategy) A Service Provider that provides IT Services to External Customers.
Underpinning Contract (UC)	(Service Design) A Contract between an IT Service Provider and a Third Party. The Third Party provides goods or Services that support delivery of an IT Service to a Customer. The Underpinning Contract defines targets and responsibilities that are required to meet agreed Service Level Targets in an SLA.
Unit Cost	(Service Strategy) The Cost to the IT Service Provider of providing a single Component of an IT Service. For example the Cost of a single desktop PC, or of a single Transaction.
Urgency	(Service Transition) (Service Design) A measure of how long it will be until an Incident, Problem or Change has a significant Impact on the Business. For example a high Impact Incident may have low Urgency, if the Impact will not affect the Business until the end of the financial year. Impact and Urgency are used to assign Priority.
Usability	(Service Design) The ease with which an Application, product, or IT Service can be used. Usability Requirements are often included in a Statement of Requirements.
Use Case	(Service Design) A technique used to define required functionality and Objectives, and to Design Tests. Use Cases define realistic scenarios that describe interactions between Users and an IT Service or other System. See Change Case.
User	A person who uses the IT Service on a day-to-day basis. Users are distinct from Customers, as some Customers do not use the IT Service directly.
User Profile (UP)	(Service Strategy) A pattern of User demand for IT Services. Each User Profile includes one or more Patterns of Business Activity.
Utility	(Service Strategy) Functionality offered by a Product or Service to meet a particular need. Utility is often summarized as "what it does". See Service Utility.
Validation	(Service Transition) An Activity that ensures a new or changed IT Service, Process, Plan, or other Deliverable meets the needs of the Business. Validation ensures that Business Requirements are met even though these may have changed since the original Design. See Verification, Acceptance, Qualification, Service Validation and Testing.
Value Chain	(Service Strategy) A sequence of Processes that creates a product or Service that is of value to a Customer. Each step of the sequence builds on the previous steps and contributes to the overall product or Service. See Value Network.

Value for Money An informal measure of Cost Effectiveness. Value for Money is often based on a comparison with the Cost of alternatives.
See Cost Benefit Analysis.

Value Network (Service Strategy) A complex set of Relationships between two or more groups or organizations. Value is generated through exchange of knowledge, information, goods or Services.
See Value Chain, Partnership.

Value on Investment (Continual Service Improvement) A measurement of the expected benefit of an
(VOI) investment. VOI considers both financial and intangible benefits.
See Return on Investment.

Variable Cost (Service Strategy) A Cost that depends on how much the IT Service is used, how many products are produced, the number and type of Users, or something else that cannot be fixed in advance.
See Variable Cost Dynamics.

Variable Cost (Service Strategy) A technique used to understand how overall Costs are impacted
Dynamics by the many complex variable elements that contribute to the provision of IT Services.

Variance The difference between a planned value and the actual measured value. Commonly used in Financial Management, Capacity Management and Service Level Management, but could apply in any area where Plans are in place.

Verification (Service Transition) An Activity that ensures a new or changed IT Service, Process, Plan, or other Deliverable is complete, accurate, Reliable and matches its Design Specification.
See Validation, Acceptance, Service Validation and Testing.

Verification and (Service Transition) The Activities responsible for ensuring that information in
Audit the CMDB is accurate and that all Configuration Items have been identified and recorded in the CMDB. Verification includes routine checks that are part of other Processes. For example, verifying the serial number of a desktop PC when a User logs an Incident. Audit is a periodic, formal check.

Version (Service Transition) A Version is used to identify a specific Baseline of a Configuration Item. Versions typically use a naming convention that enables the sequence or date of each Baseline to be identified. For example Payroll Application Version 3 contains updated functionality from Version 2.

Vision A description of what the Organization intends to become in the future. A Vision is created by senior management and is used to help influence Culture and Strategic Planning.

Vital Business (Service Design) A Function of a Business Process which is critical to the success of
Function (VBF) the Business. Vital Business Functions are an important consideration of Business Continuity Management, IT Service Continuity Management and Availability Management.

Vulnerability	A weakness that could be exploited by a Threat. For example an open firewall port, a password that is never changed, or a flammable carpet. A missing Control is also considered to be a Vulnerability.
Warm Standby	Synonym for Intermediate Recovery.
Warranty	(Service Strategy) A promise or guarantee that a product or Service will meet its agreed Requirements. See Service Validation and Testing, Service Warranty.
Work in Progress (WIP)	A Status that means Activities have started but are not yet complete. It is commonly used as a Status for Incidents, Problems, Changes etc.
Work Instruction	A Document containing detailed instructions that specify exactly what steps to follow to carry out an Activity. A Work Instruction contains much more detail than a Procedure and is only created if very detailed instructions are needed.
Workaround	(Service Operation) Reducing or eliminating the Impact of an Incident or Problem for which a full Resolution is not yet available. For example by restarting a failed Configuration Item. Workarounds for Problems are documented in Known Error Records. Workarounds for Incidents that do not have associated Problem Records are documented in the Incident Record.
Workload	The Resources required to deliver an identifiable part of an IT Service. Workloads may be Categorized by Users, groups of Users, or Functions within the IT Service. This is used to assist in analyzing and managing the Capacity, Performance and Utilization of Configuration Items and IT Services. The term Workload is sometimes used as a synonym for Throughput.

References

Bon, J. van (ed.) (2007). *Foundations of IT Service Management - based on ITIL V3.* Zaltbommel: Van Haren Publishing

Office of Government Commerce (2007). *ITIL: Continual Service Improvement.* London: The Stationary Office

Office of Government Commerce (2007). *Glossary ITIL Version 3:* http://www.best-management-practice.com

Index

ITIL Books
The Official Books from itSMF

Foundations of IT Service Management Based on ITIL®V3
Now updated to encompass all of the implications of the V3 refresh of
ITIL, the new V3 Foundations book looks at Best Practices, focusing on the
Lifecycle approach, and covering the ITIL Service Lifecycle, processes and
functions for Service Strategy, Service Design, Service Operation, Service
Transition and Continual Service Improvement.
ISBN: 978 908753057 0 (ENGLISH EDITION)
PRICE €39.95 EXCL TAX

Foundations of IT Service Management Based on ITIL®
The bestselling ITIL® V2 edition of this popular guide is available as
usual, with 13 language options to give you the widest possible global
perspective on this important subject.
ISBN: 978 907721258 5 (ENGLISH EDITION)
PRICE €39.95 EXCL TAX

IT Service Management Based on ITIL®V3: A Pocket Guide
A concise summary for ITIL®V3, providing a quick and portable reference tool to
this leading set of best practices for IT Service Management.
ISBN: 978 908753102 7 (ENGLISH EDITION)
PRICE €14.95 EXCL TAX

Van Haren Publishing (VHP) is a leading international publisher, specializing in best practice titles for IT
management and business management. VHP publishes in 14 languages, and has sales and distribution agents
in over 40 countries worldwide: www.vanharen.net

ISO/IEC 20000
The Official Books from itSMF

ISO/IEC 20000: An Introduction
Promoting awareness of the certification for organizations within the IT Service Management environment.
ISBN: 978 908753081 5 (ENGLISH EDITION)
PRICE €49.95 EXCL TAX

Implementing ISO/IEC 20000 Certification: The Roadmap
Practical advice, to assist readers through the requirements of the standard, the scoping, the project approach, the certification procedure and management of the certification.
ISBN: 978 908753082 2
PRICE €39.95 EXCL TAX

ISO/IEC 20000: A Pocket Guide
A quick and accessible guide to the fundamental requirements for corporate certification.
ISBN: 978 907721279 0 (ENGLISH EDITION)
PRICE €14.95 EXCL TAX

Other leading ITSM Books from itSMF

Metrics for IT Service Management
A general guide to the use of metrics as a mechanism to control and steer IT service organizations, with consideration of the design and implementation of metrics in service organizations using industry standard frameworks.
ISBN: 978 907721269 1
PRICE €39.95 EXCL TAX

Six Sigma for IT Management
The first book to provide a coherent view and guidance for using the Six Sigma approach successfully in IT Service Management, whilst aiming to merge both Six Sigma and ITIL® into a single unified approach to continuous improvement. Six Sigma for IT Management: A Pocket Guide is also available.
ISBN: 978 907721230 1 (ENGLISH EDITION)
PRICE €39.95 EXCL TAX

Frameworks for IT Management
An unparalleled guide to the myriad of IT management instruments currently available to IT and business managers. Frameworks for IT Management: A Pocket Guide is also available.
ISBN: 978 907721290 5 (ENGLISH EDITION)
PRICE €39.95 EXCL TAX

IT Governance based on CobiT 4.1:
A Management Guide
Detailed information on the overall process model as well as the theory behind it.
ISBN: 978 90 8753116 4 (ENGLISH EDITION)
PRICE €20,75 EXCL TAX